Executive Being

Executive Being

Humanizing Business One Leader at a Time

Katherine Lazaruk

BUSINESS EXPERT PRESS

Leader in applied, concise business books

First published in 2024 by
Business Expert Press, LLC
222 East 46th Street, New York, NY 10017
www.businessexpertpress.com

ISBN-13: 978-1-63742-714-9 (paperback)
ISBN-13: 978-1-63742-715-6 (e-book)

Business Expert Press Corporate Communication Collection

First edition: 2024

10 9 8 7 6 5 4 3 2 1

This book is dedicated to all the changemakers who dare to hope that the future of work could be kinder, gentler, and more sustainable for all

Description

Executive Presence Is Dead, Now What?

All your life you've followed the "rules" of executive presence and leadership to get where you are and suddenly they're just not working the way they used to. The business world is clamoring for authentic leadership, but you don't know what to share, what to wear, or how to show up as your "whole self," or for people bringing their "whole selves" to work. *Executive Being: Humanizing Business One Leader at a Time* has the answers.

Here's what's in it for you:

- Why we need a different kind of leader now;
- How authentic leadership outpaces stale rules of executive presence every time;
- Seven succinct practices on how to BE a good leader for a feeling world;
- Seven special appendices for my very experienced leaders.

If you're finding it's not quite as easy to lead as it was before, or you're new to leadership, it's time to try something different and to lead in a way that's true to you, for the world.

Contents

Contents

Testimonials

"I recognize the importance of doing this work and want to continue to dive in and keep the journey going, with my team and then more teams. How can we get more people doing this?"—**Kari Lockhart, Partner, Deloitte**

"The humanization approach is very important because we are dealing with brains and psychology, which are imperfect compared to a simplistic machine/robot. You've cut a huge swath with this book."—**Kursten Faller, Founder, Midgard Project Management**

"What came alive for me was the permission to be differently myself and how to understand what that is and how to create congruence."
—**Camila Merlano, Western Canada Marketing Lead, McDonalds**

"I'm not naturally drawn to poetry, but I loved the unique style and delivery, and it's a voice I haven't heard in the development space, so I have no doubt it will find your people!"—**Tom Lancaster, Founder, Altitude Evolution**

Foreword

As someone on the precipice of old-white guy-hood, I never take myself
too seriously and I like my business reading to be the same. I found this
book to be a refreshing take on a leadership style we all need to embody to
progress in a business world that is rapidly shifting. The poetry is an enjoy-
able palate cleanser between courses of hard-hitting facts and practical
tips for "getting real". It's also a lighthearted "smack in the face" for those
of us who strive to be inclusive while still challenging our employees to
showcase their abilities and unique talents.

Young people switch companies at a breakneck pace for better pay-
checks and better leadership. Retention of staff isn't about team building
events. It's more about the day-to-day and individualized leadership—letting them know you're there and you care. Humanizing your leadership
and your workplace puts you on the cutting edge of this new model, and
it will set you apart from thousands of old-school leaders that wonder
why their people won't work (for them).

Katherine hits the nail on the head here. The age-old leadership model
is shifting, and we, more experienced leaders, need to up our game and
shift our own practice to meet it, starting with embracing and accepting
our own unique self-expression. Employee retention is no joke and if
we can't learn to embrace the differences that young people bring to the
table, free of prejudice, our businesses will fail to adapt and will suffer as
a result. As she says, "the best organizations are built on relationships, not
hierarchy."

Success will not happen if we can't relate to our key players; we can't
use the "I'm too busy" excuse any more to avoid investing in that connection and healthy company culture that empowered people who bring
their "whole selves" to work creates. Even your dress code (I personally
love jeans and a t-shirt) can shift to reflect the progress we need to make as
a society. I know that surrounding myself with different types of leaders,
women, men, anyone who embraces the idea of progress and evolution, is

what will carry our organization through difficult times, changing market and consumer needs, and on to sustained success.

The truth is, I've read a lot of business books, and this is the most interesting and playful one I've seen in a while. If you're ready for real change, buckle up and read on.

—Ryan Benn, CEO of Alive Publishing Group Inc.

Acknowledgments

I would like to acknowledge the village without whom my books would never be written and released into the wild, including my writing coach and fairy godmother, Tina Overbury, my faithful first readers who are always kind and fair, my writing group of amazing women, my good friends who provide continuous acceptance and encouragement, and finally, my husband, David, who loves me dearly every day. Thanks also to Alan Weiss for his good connections and to Scott Isenberg and the team at Business Expert Press for taking a chance on a new voice. I am very grateful for this opportunity.

A Note on Reading This Book

Before you dive in, I want you to know that this book isn't quite like other standard corporate business books. If you bring your corporate brain to it, it's possible that you might be a little annoyed or even frustrated by the poetry and arty bits, but this is not a bad thing. Having a little bit of openness to a different kind of expression is exactly the right state to be in for taking in the messages in this book, so you're on the right track. This book is also divided into two parts, one of philosophy in Chapters 1 through 5 and the second of practices to help you begin your work in Chapters 6 through 9, so be prepared to dig in and do some work when you get there.

If, in the course of your reading, you're struggling at all with any of the bits, I invite you to try a few different ways to approach this material, to experiment with the way you take in this book, even if you don't consider yourself an artist or appreciator of art, or if you haven't been "arty" yourself. Of course, you're more than welcome to read the book any way you wish, but if you find yourself irked, perhaps you might like to try some different techniques including:

- Reading it aloud (particularly the poetry, as it has its own kind of rhythm)
- Reading it in tiny pieces
- Jumping around a bit to what resonates based on section titles
- Approaching this like a fun game instead of a straight up task or chore
- Writing in the book or highlighting with color
- Doodling or drawing pictures in the margins and white space

This approach isn't play for play's sake—it's a way of experiencing and thinking about how we learn, not just how we work. In my workshops, I often use color and play—for example, when a client gets stuck on a brainstorm or a plan, I invite them to use a different colored marker, which is a signal to their brains that something has changed and it usually leads to a new tangent or flow that helps move the project forward. In this book, I invite you to take an "enjoy the doing" approach versus a "get it done" approach and I think you'll find the experience more pleasurable. Finally, if you still aren't sure how to read the poems or hear them in your mind, you can always look me up on Audible and find some of my other audiobook samples to give you the idea of my style. Unless you're in the audiobook of this one. Then you'll be fine. Have fun!

A special note for all my experienced leaders who are successful in the current system:

I've written a few cheeky appendixes for you at the back and you may wish to jump to those first because it's not so easy to be a voice of experience in a world that's changing how it views experience. If you choose to keep reading without reading them first, please do hold on to the book because I'm about to say some things you might not like.

This book is not

This book is not
for you,
dear reader,

IF

You are looking
for the same
old
frames,
glasses seeing through
hierarchical lenses of
silos, separate and
only stock shareholder
success,

BUT

dear reader,
this book is
for you,
absolutely

IF

You are ready
for something
entirely different,
individualmeasured and
collectiveproductive and
(I daresay)

WORTHY WORK!

Come along and see
with me,
what's beyond
executivepresence
businessframeworks
strategytactics,
metrical,
KPI performance, and
the pain of working,
humans in an
inhuman world, suppressed,

BUT

changing, thank god
(or heavenkarmawhatever)

and so, dear reader

IF

you've been tired of
the rats and
the race and
the unreasonable pace of
one person doing not one,
but two or three jobs,
workloading,
expectations unrealistic, and
exhaustion so deep,
burning out the candles
one by one, falling, then

This book is for you.

If you're looking for a quick fix

If you're looking for a quick fix, put this book down immediately. I mean, yes, there are some good techniques in the final chapters that can work quickly to drive change, but in my experience, this kind of work takes time and requires some thinking and feeling and practice in order to work, particularly in workplaces that have leaned heavily on traditional organizational models. So, if you're someone who has a quick fix way of thinking and you want to jump to a solution without following the path of progression, I'm gonna just say it …

Get out now,

unless…

- You're tired of the expectations and rules for executive presence and business that leadership books and coaches and consultants have been laying out since Dale Carnegie started his gig back in 1936.
- You know there is something different coming but aren't sure what it is.
- You sense the model is breaking.
- You're excited about what is next.
- You're mad (or a little hot and bothered) about the state of work and the world.

because…

we're on a bumpy ride into another major shift in the way we work, and we don't need more of the status quo. We need leaders who are complete (I'll get to that), principled (because f&%* those can-kickers), and responsible stewards of power (not just in it for themselves). We need a new way of being, not just doing.

Get ready to do the work, or you're not going to get what you need from it, my friend.

Seriously though, if you're not ready for a shift, you're not ready—you can read on as an observer, or put this book back on the shelf for a time when it calls to you again. Be gentle.

…

…

…

Still here?
I'm glad.
You're brave.
We need you.
Let's get to it.

We've changed, the world has changed and our leadership measures and methods just haven't kept up.

You know it, or you're starting to feel it. Those little whispers of "no one wants to work" or "I can't get people back in the office." The rise of mental health issues. The polarization of the workplace and the world. The calling out of behaviors that would have been acceptable just 5 or 10 years ago. You're starting to see the damage the current system is inflicting. You've seen it before, on the face of every person who has ever been passed over for promotion because they didn't "fit the mold"—every woman who was told she slept her way to the top, every man whose introspection was mistaken for weakness, and every LGBTQIA2S+, disabled, neurodivergent, fat, or BIPOC (Black, Indigenous, People of Color) person whose identity was out front, openly challenging the status quo. Now you're seeing it in more places, with more people, and hearing little rumbles even from some of those who have been quite successful. We're moving into a different time.

This book is for the courageous.

It is for the ones who see that some of our most prominent leadership has become unbalanced, irresponsible to, and disconnected from the people they purport to lead. We see it playing out on the larger political stage and in the microcosm of small business and even in our own lives as we might struggle with exhaustion and burnout. This book is for all those who have noticed the shift and want something else for themselves and for the people under their care. It is for all who wish to become responsible stewards of power and to lead themselves and their organizations from a place of a different kind of strength, those who wish to be whole.

It's not going to be painless, because big change can hurt, but you're comfortable with that.

(clearly, or you would have dropped this book like a hot potato by now).

It will hurt, a little, or maybe a lot, depending on who you were before this.

(if you go to the gym—and I *know* you go to the gym—you know what I mean).

It will change you.

(and more importantly, since corporations are run by people, and since corporations rule the world, it can change the world too, if you're willing).

All around us we see the effects of leaders who haven't had the deep integrity to handle the toughest issues, who aren't willing to risk their own careers to do the hard things, and just keep kicking the can down the road, hoping someone else will clean up the mess. All they're looking for is another term, another contract, and another golden handshake.

We've been at the mercy of what is expedient, not what is excellent.

- We're trapped in doingdoingdoing.
- We're stuck with metrics that don't really measure success.

We're settling for a gutless version of leadership that's based on "executive presence" tips and tricks that mask who we really are and how we really feel.

- We're running way too fast and burning out, for all the wrong reasons.
- We're driving ourselves and the planet straight off the cliff of existence, patting ourselves on the back for having a nice car while we do it.

What if, instead of ramping up, we took a U-turn?

Let's get real.

CHAPTER 1

Get Real

A Lot Is Going Wrong Right Now

(and we have an opportunity to really make it right...)

Get real*

"Get real!" he said to me,
years ago, when I suggested that
something could be different,
ideal, aspirational vibe, and
stuck behind the old paradigm,
peeking out from the corners,
fearful of loss, of lack, of
stepping out tall poppy to be
struck down by the cruelty of
the world we've allowed them to build
on our backs, he said,
"Get real!"
and I thought,

"I will, but not the way you think."

---

* I just love how "Get real!" is sometimes thrown like a sharp left hook at those of us who dare to imagine the world could be different than it is, don't you?

May I speak plainly?

Our leadership model is broken. You know it, I know it, we all know it. It's so broken that we have to break ourselves to keep it going, to fit. How many times have you heard someone say they were burned out, exhausted, or deeply unhappy in spite of outward material success? I know that in my practice, I see a lot of really caring leaders who just can't keep up with the ever-increasing demands on their time, attention, and energy. Though they're outwardly at the top of their game, they're not happy. What I've noticed is that we've collectively spent a long time pretending that the way the world currently works is the way it should continue to work. Some of us are so deeply invested in this myth that we have a hard time adapting to the idea that "being different" is already here. You can feel it in the rumbles of anxiety at work, meltdowns in the break room, in mass resignations, and near outright revolt.

The business model is shifting.

As much as we might want to believe otherwise, we are living in deeply disconnected times. We're apart from the land that sustains us (most people don't even know where their food comes from), apart from one another (so many wars, so much conflict), and apart from ourselves (mental health issues, anyone?). Some of our wealthiest citizens are busy setting up missions to colonize planets and build metaverses, trying to get away from the reality that we can't continue on the way we have, following old pathways because we hear too many voices telling us that "this is just the way the world works." In order to survive this increasingly inhuman, machinelike trajectory of growth and efficiency, we've spent so long putting on corporate faces (*company faces*) to get through our day, that we are starting to believe our stories about the facades we construct and why. We're exhausting ourselves to keep up appearances and pretending, but the edifices are starting to crumble and soon will be tumbling.

We can't continue to run away from being human.

This might sound odd coming from a recovering executive presence coach who has made a good living doing image work that starts on the surface, but since you've picked up the book, I'm going to talk to you like I do to my clients.

"Get real!" in my world means:

- I can't help you look better without helping you be better. That's an inside job.
- I can't help you hold on to your teams until your organization is better. That's the real test of leadership.
- I can't help you (and this book won't help you) until you're willing to dig deep into what makes you and the people around you tick.

Until you make a genuine connection to yourself, your work, and your world, you're never going to be real. If we can't connect to ourselves, we can't connect to others and if we can't connect, we can't solve any of our real-world issues.

Instead of running away from our humanness, let's pull a one-eighty, and embrace it.

Let's BE.

This is table stakes. Wanna play?

What does it mean?

What does it mean
to be real
in this context of
businesscapital,
subject to numbers
(allaboutthemoney)
excelling at
growth, growth, growth?
It's been bidsellbide
your time,
for an awful, long time,
pay your dues
and wait for opportunity to
find you
IF
you fit the check box
they're boxing you in,
(hidinghiding)
BUT
if you're real, really real,
it means you're you,
no filters, no tidy files,
gifted with all
you got for free,
free to
say what you really think and
no more hiding and
FINALLY
you're seen,
heard,
valued,
(maybe not in your current role
but somewhere, where they see

the real you.)
And the cost?
Maybe you'll lose
that promotion but
keep your integrity.
Maybe you'll lose the
efficient in favor of the effective.
Maybe you'll get promoted but
for all the right reasons, because
you can care, when you're real,
really present and there for
what makes the business go
round and round,
for the people who do all the
thingsandthings,
and for you, to find your
purposehappiness presence.
This care,
my friend,
is REAL.

Real is no bulls%$#, someone who is consistently themselves, no matter the situation.

They might turn the volume on their personality up or down, like a speaker. They might show you a different facet here and there, like a jewel in new lighting. They are who they are, no matter what. You're never surprised (except pleasantly) by someone who is real. Real doesn't hide, it doesn't act in artificial ways, and real shows its genuine personality. When real people experience an emotion attached to a situation, we can see that it's happening. If they have thoughts or ideas, they are transparent. The "poker face" game of concealing, consciously or unconsciously, what they truly think or feel disappears. They say what they perceive to be true. They act in ways that are truthful to who they are.

May I speak plainly?

- *Pretending to be something we're not to succeed is exhausting.*
- *How freeing would it be if you could bring your real, whole self to the office?*
- *How connected could we be to others if they could be themselves, too?*

When you're real, you can really care and you can really connect. It's risky, because we've been penalized for telling the truth in the past, BUT...

This is not a reason to retreat. It's a reason to move forward.

The self/other component

The self/other component
(get real)
is composite, composed of
self and other,
aware, and
we all want to act
not react
(eventually).
To get real, we
have to know ourselves,
let down our walls and
live with the idea that
we might, just might, be
human after all and
when we know ourselves
we can know others better
because compassion
(opening space)
makes space
for youmeusall to
be known, and
when we're known
we can more easily know,
move at the speed of trust
(so fast)
that lasts, at last and
lets us move
in short spurts and
long strides and
do things well and sweetly,
together.
Unhidden and bidden, we
can sit with the unknown,
unknowable and

paradoxical, the profit
(all around, not just money)
goes up when we work
together.
Speed like lightning,
the sparkly kind, not rushed,
just naturally moved, this
selfother chemistry lights our
work afire and, fired up, we burn
bright, light, and can you imagine
how well a business would go,
(and the world at large)
if we all knewknow each other
for real?

Becoming acutely aware of ourselves and others in the environments we inhabit is the first small step to being the kind of leader we need now.

Instead of zoning out, numbing, what if we spent some time tuning in?

One of the key issues that many of my clients face is the desire to stop or slow the barrage of requirements that seems to increase daily. They sometimes need to numb out, choosing to lose themselves in scrolling, drinking, or other activities that help blunt the emotional impact of their daily lives. They've needed to "not feel" in order to survive their corporate environment and some of them have adopted less healthy strategies to compartmentalize and keep things bottled up. Others have adopted socially acceptable addictions such as hyper exercise, rigid control of their schedules and diet, or working unreasonably long hours. Once we start the work together, they begin to see the value of slowing down and noticing what's happening, enabling them to step away from numbing and into nourishment on a sustainable basis. I invite you to imagine the results for you, your organization, and the world if we adopted this "tuning in" wholesale.

May I speak plainly?

- *What if we stopped for a moment or five, and paid closer attention to what was really happening with ourselves and with others?*
- *What if we could truly identify what made us tick and then adjust our course and environment so those things matched our pace?*
- *What if we leaned into awareness, both of self and others?*

Let's Talk Awareness

At the risk of being pedantic, but in the interest of making sure we're all on the same page while reading, let me state what I mean by "aware." I like to keep it simple and use the standard dictionary definition.

Aware: Having or showing realization, perception, or knowledge.

While it's great to be aware, there's a substantial difference between just having or showing it and living into it. If we're really aware, we don't just know about something, we practice it daily. We are thinking not only of our own perceptions, realizations, and knowledge but also thinking of our relationship to all of those things and our relationship to the perceptions, realizations, and knowledge of others at the same time. If we have this level of awareness, we can use it to navigate the sensitivities of people as they come into the workplace, rather than cutting them off in favor of "professionalism" and "performance." Every single person with whom we come in contact has a whole emotional life, past trauma and a set of life circumstances that either made it easier or more difficult for them to be in the room with you now. Imagine we could activate this level of awareness, and understand the differences in context that we each bring to the table. Imagine we can create a workplace where you and others are truly seen, heard, and valued, and allowed to feel what you feel and think what you think for a moment. Consider what that might do for the effectiveness of our work. Your first reaction might be to think it would get messy and you're not wrong, but I think we need to abandon this idea that messy is wrong. Messy is just a moment we can move through when we're looking at the inside job of our own work to BE executives, not just DO executive things. On this journey, more awareness is better than less and we need it in two flavors: self and other.

What Does It Mean to Be Self-Aware?

In her book, *Insight*, organizational psychologist Tasha Eurich estimates that only 10 to 15 percent of the population is truly aware.[1] She talks about internal awareness, the knowledge we have of ourselves, and our ability to recognize our own values, motivations, and aspirations, as well as external awareness, or the ability to understand how we're perceived by others.

Awareness is taking a journey with ourselves, digging deep into what formed us, what we believe from that formation or don't, of crafting our own values and crafting our lives to fit. It's connecting to our values (which might be outside the current dominant paradigm or culture) and then acting in accordance with the values we hold. It's learning enough about ourselves so we know (or have a pretty good idea of) how we'll react to or handle the unknown. It's seeking to understand our own internal landscape, and learning what we need to do to care for ourselves. It's knowing ourselves so well that we know, down in our bones, that we are doing the right thing at the right moment, and that we can adapt and handle anything that comes our way and regulate our emotions and thoughts in as many situations as possible. Without self-awareness, we can't direct our personal efforts effectively. We might react emotionally, shut down or flare up with anger, and lose our minds when we get feedback or encounter unfamiliar things. When that happens, we miss a lot and can't take on new information to grow.

What Does It Mean to Be Aware of Others?

Being aware of others means being able to consciously recognize and acknowledge the existence, experiences, emotions, and needs of people who are not you.

This can be the tougher level of awareness to achieve, particularly if you've been successful operating in the current system and have expected all others to adjust as you did. It can be hard to listen to the experiences of others and not dismiss them as simply lazy or otherwise. To achieve this level of other awareness, you need the ability not just to hear, but to attune to other perspectives, feelings, and circumstances. You need to imagine yourself in their shoes and try to see their filters. When you're other-aware, you can listen, read social cues, observe body language, and interpret these things effectively. Using these skills, you can understand the ways people relate to one another and actively seek to empathize with their unique identities and journeys and find ways to relate to them in the workplace and the world. Without both dimensions of awareness, we can't connect with ourselves or anyone else.

More than observation, awareness is about cultivating genuine interest in and consideration for the well-being and happiness of ourselves and others in our world at the same time.

With these two types of awareness at play, we can experience significant benefits. We can have more respectful and effective conversations and interactions. We can build communities at work and in the world that are harmonious and inclusive. For us to work together, we need to align or overlap mental frameworks. We need to calibrate our values with others' values, where possible, and we need to be able to relate when there's a mismatch of values. Without both self and other awareness, we can't hold space for different perspectives. Our ego jumps up and causes us to clutch our own views more closely. We find it harder to collaborate.

Without self and other awareness, there can be no progress.

By now, if you're an experienced leader, you know this seems obvious. Most of us who lead or aspire to lead get this part, or we wouldn't have attained our current levels of success. Unfortunately, the reality is we still have a lot of leaders who are just getting by on authority and, frankly, some who are successful in name only. They've got the fancy title, but are terrible leaders in practice. You know it, I know it. We've all seen it time and time again. Here's the thing, even for most of us who have been leading for a while.

We often get *just aware enough* to do the job.

We work on this just enough so we can understand ourselves and others on a superficial level, but we don't stop to understand ourselves or others in depth, often because we feel we can't. We think there's too much to do, too many deadlines, too much shareholder pressure, and too many rungs on the ladder to climb. We get on the "success track" and often don't stop to question where we're going or why, until we're running smack into the wall of misery. We're either quietly miserable, enduring the small slow pains of daily life, or loudly crashing and losing our sh*& or simply burning out, just from trying to survive like machines and stay on the surface.

What if we did business based on our capacity for deep humanity, instead of pretending we're not human at all?

What if it could **BE** different?

CHAPTER 2

Getting Real When It Comes to Business

The best organizations

The best organizations
are built on relationships,
not hierarchy, and
to get there
you have to work through
what happens when
whole selves show up at the
boardroom table—sure, we need a
few leadership roles here and there but
in the buck stops here-ness only,
because we can't work things out if we don't
relate
and we miss a lot when we don't
listen.
Consider stepping out of your role,
status stated,
and start
relating.

Leadership isn't just for the old guard anymore.

I'm not opposed to the old guard; I love my old guard leaders, especially the ones who work hard with me to stay relevant, accepting, kind, and decent, to achieve deeper levels of awareness and who are interested in getting real. These are the ones who realize the importance of stepping aside and preparing the way for what's new. We need their voices of experience in our rooms. However, I do like to poke the other ones who rely heavily on positional power, past paradigms, authority, and traditional education to lead. I think they need a little poke every now and then.* We need leaders who are plugged in, who see that things are shifting, and who are able to connect. We need to connect.

Real connection to ourselves, to one another, and to our systems drives better results than clinging to outdated systems.

> *Poke: Especially when they're the ones running around acting like nothing has changed, trying to control everybody, pushing people off their land, fighting over resources, building rockets and substandard subs, creating endless war, and not spending money on things that matter, such as living wages, benefits, education, health care, housing, food, and community building. When they're acting like the world is their private Monopoly game, they need more than a poke. They need to be voted out of office, retired out of the C-suite and out of their ivory towers, taken off podcasts, and off pulpits, sat down in circles together, and schooled on how to care for the finite nature of things, themselves, and others until they can be relevant, accepting, decent, and kind.**
>
> **Poke poke: If you **are** an old guard leader, and feeling a bit injured and stereotyped on reading this, or thinking about how it's unfair that you're being characterized as part of the problem when you're trying hard to keep up and what you think we really need is diversity of thought, please do see the **appendixes** at the end of this book if you didn't read them when I suggested them in the beginning. They really will help, I promise.

Companies that embrace different kinds of leaders consistently outperform those that don't.

But don't just take my word for it...

- McKinsey & Company's Diversity Matters Report from 2015 found a statistically significant relationship between a more diverse leadership team and financial outperformance. Companies in the top quartile for gender diversity were 15 percent more likely to have financial returns above their national industry median.[2]
- Boston Consulting Group's 2017 survey found that companies with above-average diversity on their leadership teams reported innovation revenue that was 19 percentage points higher than that of companies with below-average leadership diversity.[3]
- Deloitte's Global Human Capital Trends Report from 2020 found that inclusive organizations are six times more likely to be innovative and agile, eight times more likely to achieve better business outcomes, and twice as likely to meet or exceed financial targets.[4]

The trouble with finding diverse leaders is that the leaders we're looking for don't fit the standards we've set for what good leadership looks like.

The Paradox of Perception

Imagine that you're at a conference and a speaker takes the stage to talk about the latest innovations in business. The speaker is young, female and has a very high-pitched nasally voice. She's wearing a very feminine, slightly flamboyant floral dress and stands out in a sea of navy, gray, and black suits. Her hair is long and curled over her shoulders. She's wearing three-inch heels, brightly colored and bedazzled with rhinestones. Or a speaker who is heavily tattooed, with piercings and punk hair in a band, tee shirt, and jeans. Or a short, heavyset nonbinary person with a sharply angled haircut, wearing a tailored suit jacket with a tulle skirt and combat boots.

What is your immediate reaction? Be honest.

Chances are you're going to have to mentally and emotionally work hard to discard your thoughts about their appearance and voice to hear the intelligent, thoughtful concepts they're outlining. This is the paradox of perception. How much information are we missing from one another, just because the person who is speaking or writing does not fit our image of what a credible source looks, feels, or sounds like? If the speakers in our example shrank themselves or changed themselves to fit an existing paradigm, part of their message would be lost. Paradoxically, we need to take ourselves out of our old framework and be present with the people in front of us to hear something new. Be careful not to discard a message simply because it's not being presented in a way that you would normally hear or because it elicits a strong reaction for you.

As people bring their whole selves to work more often, we need to learn to see the message and the messenger without prejudice.

This means that the perceptions of what makes for a good executive presence are changing and we need to change along with them.

Where we've been is

Where we've been is
a sh*%showhorror of
overgrowth, uncalibrated,
elusive quality seeking the
pinnacle of what leadership
looks like, or should, and
all the books that are being written today
are the same books that were written
away, years before, tired platitudes,
beatitudes of boredom, and all
the "old white guy" tropes, but
the world has moved on and modernized so
why aren't we looking at what's next for
executive presence too?

There's No "One-Size-Fits-All" Definition

In our quest to understand what good leadership looks like, we often look to past experts for definitions on "executive presence." If you search online for a book on executive presence, you'll find titles that sound like "Unlocking Executive Presence," "Mastering the Art of Executive Presence," or "The Executive Presence Code." All of them promise to reveal the secrets to becoming a leader of influence, but if you were to do a side-by-side comparison, you'd realize they are just variations on a theme, not entirely new compositions. Even the newest, "new rules of executive presence" barely give a nod to change. In fact, try asking a few people for an explanation of executive presence. You'll generally get vague answers that will include a set of words in common such as charisma, confidence, assertiveness, gravitas, or decisiveness. Executive presence is mostly something that goes by "feel." Though it has a series of actions one can perform to demonstrate it, it's little more than a prescribed and uniform veneer that's useful in the current system.

While the systems remain the same, the same tricks will work... for a while,

BUT...

The trouble with executive presence

The trouble with executive presence,
you see, is that it doesn't
see what is, that is.
It misses all the artful heartful parts of
all the people who never fit the mold,
old moldy stale, sold a baker's dozen
bill of goods, floured dusty and
caked with the patriarchy,
burnished bronze, baked
in the fires of all the rules
we had to bend, and break
to fit and sit and stay in place.
Never ours,
the hours!
Time wasted, the ways to churn and burn
waisted belts buckled, collared, tied,
the people resources spent,
human capital wrenched,
benched, burned out, and told,
"You weren't successful."
"You'd never be."

If you didn't, couldn't, wouldn't
follow the rules meant, written, for
husbands with wives to burden bear,
kept safe and scared, scarred,
invisible labor holding up all
the pillars of the earth, capitalized,
and any unique you queued up
went down in flames of executive
presence and all the books they're writing now,
repeating, rebeating,

(dead horses)
were written then and back then
and now?
No.
We know.
There's something more.

Before We Get to "More," Let's Look at "Less"

Executive presence has for years been revered as essential for success in leadership roles and has been described as a combination of charisma, confidence, and gravitas. We all know people who we would describe as having "executive presence" and there are countless "experts" out there who can tell you what techniques to practice getting it. The problem is the books that are being written now are essentially the same books that were written 30 years ago and all of the characteristics they outline are based on the ways people who are successful in the current system behave.

The current standards for executive presence are subjective at best and harmful at worst.

They are inherently biased, based on old-paradigm thinking, and rife with all the "isms." If we are to move to a kind of presence that is truthful and grounded, we have to challenge the prevailing notions of what constitutes strong executive presence and think about how they perpetuate systemic inequality. For example, an oft-used current direction in presentation is "speak low and slow." This refers to lowering the pitch of your voice and slowing down the pace of your communication. While I understand the slowing down part, as speed sometimes impedes clarity, the "lower pitch" part is directly derived from our model of male leadership. Voice pitch influences the perception of leadership capacity in both men and women.

At the risk of repeating myself, don't just take my word for it...

- A study in the U.S. National Library of Medicine from 2012 established that while people are free to choose their leaders, these choices cannot be understood in isolation from biological factors.[5]
- In 2016, an article published in the *Journal of Experimental Psychology* found that, in a decision-making activity, people who lowered the pitch of their voice were considered more dominant and of higher rank.[6]

(Unfortunately, many studies have also found that men find women with higher pitched voices more attractive, so it's a classic double bind for women, which happens far more than we know.)

While voice pitch might seem to be a very small detail, it's part of the whole system of definition of presence as seen through a model of male, often white leadership. We see it in other places too, not just in the pitch of voices. In terms of professional appearance, all you need to do is Google it and you'll find countless images of white faces. Google the opposite, "unprofessional appearance" and you'll predominantly find faces of color. Even the way we dress is coded for male dominance, with dark suits and white shirts being evaluated as the most professional clothing for executives. If we truly want diverse leadership, we need to divest from these old-school social markers that keep us blind to leadership potential in other forms.

Let's look at all three characteristics typically considered to be essential to having a strong executive presence:

Confidence is considered a core component of executive presence, but it is viewed through a gendered lens. The standard for confidence is rooted in examples from male leadership, coded in command and control. Studies consistently show that women who assert themselves in the workplace are often perceived as aggressive or overly ambitious. This double standard restricts the way women can express confidence, forcing them to navigate a narrow path to executive presence. To redefine executive presence, we must first acknowledge that confidence is not the sole domain of men and that diverse expressions of confidence should be celebrated.

Charisma is another pillar of executive presence, but its definition has been shaped by stereotypes rooted in the existing examples of leadership. We often associate charisma with extroverted, gregarious individuals who fit the mold of the "ideal" leader. This stereotype is culturally based and excludes introverts, those with different communication styles, and individuals from marginalized communities. By deconstructing the conventional view of charisma, we can recognize that there are many ways to be magnetic and influential in leadership roles.

Finally, gravitas, often defined as dignity, seriousness, and importance, is seen as a cornerstone of executive presence. However, the standards for gravitas prioritize rigid, emotionless expressions of authority that align with traditional male leadership. To break free from these constraints, we must expand our understanding of gravitas to include a wider range of emotional expressions and leadership styles.

We must challenge the notion that one size fits all and embrace diversity in leadership.

The ability to connect authentically with others and display empathy should be seen as strength, not weakness.

And What About the Way Leaders Look?

Executive presence is not limited to behavior; it also includes the way we look. Even here, the standards are heavy with bias. Our ideal leadership "look" in North America is generally thin, white, well-dressed in tailored clothing with smooth lines, low color and high contrast, and tall, usually named John. (I'm joking a little bit with the idea that our ideal is named John, but it was only in 2023 that women CEOs finally outnumbered CEOs named John).[7] Dress codes often favor these types of conservative Western norms that are uncomfortable or irrelevant to many people, especially now. Though the standard levels of formality in clothing are shifting as the work environment becomes more casual, these standards can still be especially alienating to anyone who doesn't quite fit them: people with different body types, non-Western people, those from nonwhite backgrounds, transgender individuals, and people who defy other norms.

Dress code rules of

Dress code rules of
etiquette tick ticking away on my
heart and mind, divine but
exclusionary first and now
intrusive dividing our
hearts and minds and
love, we need you to come and
love us into ourselves and our little rules,
tea party fun, five years old, and it's all a game of
pretend and so now we get to pretend
something else, new, different,
colorful and alive and wild and free and exciting,
hippie dip, Haight Ashbury wild, but not so far from
Wall Street suits and gaming the games of
stocks, bonded and joy,
in the ups downs, crashes and booms of
illusory money agreed social conventions soul contracts and
what the f&%# is it all anyway, we just decide,
so who decided this?
Let's decide something new.

May I speak plainly?

- *To challenge these biases in appearance, we first have to know and accept they exist.*
- *We then need to see that different styles of dress and presentation can still convey professionalism and competence.*
- *A more inclusive view of appearance allows individuals to express their identity authentically and helps us connect with one another.*

The standards of the executive presence coaching of the past are especially hard on those who have multiple intersecting, marginalized identities. For example, a queer person of color may be up against compounded biases, which makes it even more challenging for them to conform to traditional norms of leadership (e.g., black hairstyles are less professional, African American Vernacular English (AAVE) is less professional, and LGBTQ folks are not safe—yes, people still think these heinous things, consciously or unconsciously, depending on their upbringing). When we acknowledge that identities are complex and affected by many things, we can start dismantling the old rigid standards and start shaping something that works for everyone. Leaders should be celebrated for their unique experiences and perspectives, not held to a one-size-fits-all model that favors the privileged.

I saw a sea of

I saw a sea of
blue and caramel
suits and shoes
yesterday,
wave after wave
breaking on the
sparkling pavement,
stone shores, concrete
oceans moving to
the tide of conferences,
scheduled crowds and
though their movement
was beautiful, flocking
murmuring flow,
just once I wished to see
a sea of saris, sarongs, or
high–low fashion to
single out of
group embrace of
individuals, whole and
see appetizer-sized servings
of who they really are
underneath
all
that
blue.
Caramel.

The evolutionary advantages of fitting in are falling away.

More than just a desire for connection and expression, we now have research to support the advantages of diversity and acceptance and how it affects our hearts and minds and we need to start moving toward a place of both.

We need better social contracts.

Historically, leadership has been equated with masculinity and whiteness, creating an enduring template that excludes those who do not conform. Consider the image of the stoic, strong, and decisive leader—often a white, heterosexual man—as the archetype of executive presence. This image not only excludes women, LGBTQ+ individuals, and people of color but also perpetuates the idea that these qualities are inherent in certain groups and absent in others.

We need to change the box, not keep trying to fit inside it.

Unique self-expression is a vehicle for cultivating and leveraging a strong presence in leadership and in leadership development. As we move to a more authentic model, we need pathways for understanding and adapting to more authentic leaders.

It's time to find new ways to describe good leaders and to help leverage uniqueness instead of conformity.

Coming out

Coming out
of an industrialized age,
where every bolt
had to be in the
same place,
same way,
every time,
precisely,
we learned to act
in mechanized ways,
dehumanizing ourselves,
stripping away the change,
unique, from piece to piece, and
now, moving to the
information age,
connected,
we must reconnect those
ancient switches that
were with us long before machines
(lingering) and
find our way back to our
naturalanimalselves, soulsome,
elevating our brains
(conscious)
catch the vibe of
the moments
small and large
(moving) and
be, be, busy,
like busy bees,
follow,
a divine order

(no hurry)
in time, leaning
in,
on,
up,
(not only) but
into,
ourselves,
each other, and
life.

In trying to meet these standards for executive presence, too many of us, for too long, have played by these rules at work. We've been taught that fitting in is what will make us successful and for a long time it's worked, for some of us, but it isn't working anymore. We can't afford to sit around and continue to pretend that we're somehow separate from one another. There are too many indicators now, and too many studies that show that workplaces that don't actively work toward accepting a variety of unique personality types are at both an economic and social disadvantage.

On the economic front, we see some of the largest costs mount in things such as increased employee turnover, decreased employee engagement, less innovation and creativity, a lack of psychological safety, and low workforce morale. Underrepresentation of diverse people leads to many feeling undervalued, unheard, or excluded. This causes them to either stay and be miserable, because they don't have the economic opportunity to leave, or to go to other opportunities, leaving the cost of their replacement with their employers. I love attaching a hard dollar cost to these things but, weirdly as I was researching, I found that the exact dollar cost was hard to pin down with a solid citation. What I can tell you is that the estimates from studies by Gallup and other reputable organizations were astronomical, most ranging in the billions of dollars. Billions, with a B.

Conformity exacts a steep price, and the trade-off of traditionally defined success isn't always enough anymore.

The pressure to conform to biased standards of executive presence takes a toll on mental health. Women, people of color, LGBTQ+ individuals, and others who do not fit the traditional mold often face what is commonly called imposter syndrome,* anxiety, and stress as they navigate

---

* Fun fact: Imposter syndrome isn't a real thing—it's a media mess based on a very specific study from the 1970s that followed some high achievers that, *despite all the evidence to the contrary*, absolutely *could not* accept their skills, talents, and gifts. As usual, the media grabbed something highly specific that exists in a very tiny subset of leaders, generalized it, pathologized it, and made it an industry. We all experience insecurity from time to time. It's not a "syndrome." Unfortunately, making it a "syndrome" is catchy and bankable, so we keep seeing people making

workplaces that demand conformity. To promote inclusivity and well-being, we must prioritize mental health support, challenge biased standards, and create environments where everyone can thrive without compromising their authenticity.

Rethinking executive presence is not about lowering standards but expanding them.

May I speak plainly?

- *We are pretending that leaders only speak, look, think, and behave one way.*
- *We need to get reconnected with our individuality, our humanity, and manage it all collectively.*
- *We don't have to hide our punk hair, full skirts, and rhinestone-heeled selves in navy suits anymore.*

AND...

We've got a little work to do.

---

money off something that doesn't really exist. You might feel a normal amount of insecurity in situations where the stakes are high or you're new, but you definitely don't have anything like the pathological lack of belief in yourself demonstrated by those specific study participants. I reiterate—it's not a syndrome. You're experiencing a normal human emotion, not a lethal condition. It's. Not. A. Thing.

CHAPTER 3

We've Got Some Walls in the Way

We've gotten good at building

We've gotten good at building
walls, wars,
wigglingwrecking our way
out of our connections
to others, pretending
our stories
are the only ones
that matter.

The biggest challenge we face now is strengthening our ability to connect effectively with others.

Our work lives and our personal lives are more integrated than ever before. With the rise of remote and hybrid work, we've gotten a glimpse into each others' personal lives in ways that weren't possible when we went to the office and could pretend we were fine, that our outward image was entirely accurate. I think the most humanizing (and refreshing) thing we've seen over the past few years with our lives on video is realizing that none of us live an entirely clutter free, perfectly tucked up and curated life. We're finally getting to see other parts of the world, things that we could previously comfortably, if not morally, ignore, tucked up on our couches, in our homes and cars, insulated by wealth and privilege. We're seeing cracks everywhere, not just in our own lives. We're coming to understand that we inhabit a finite system that can't continue with infinite growth, so we need to look inward.

Everything in our social media, political landscape, and bumpy ride to the future is calling us to get *more* connected, not less.

BUT…

Embracing connection, real connection, has some real barriers.

Speed

This whole global connection thing has come at us so fast, with so many people and a whole world thrown at us, that we seem to be unable to process all the connections we need to make, as quickly as we need to make them.

We need to get truly connected, not just Internet connected…

One of my favorite colleagues from London, Sarah Brummitt (she's a force of nature, check her out), often says:

"The pace of change has never been this fast, and it will never be this slow again."

The world is running hot, literally. Things are coming at us at breakneck speed. This naturally makes us want to seek quick solutions, to amp up our production, to hasten through our days to cram in as much activity as possible, just to keep up. Unfortunately, this often has the opposite effect.

We zone out to handle the pace.

We numb ourselves with scrolling, with food, with a glass of wine or two at night to "unwind." We turn off our screens when what we're seeing makes us cringe, feel discomfort, or recoil in horror. We gorge on reality TV and gossip. We build superficial connections with friends and colleagues or even strangers. We rally around causes, or celebrities, so we can feel like we belong somewhere. We exchange a few words in passing, or none, with the people we meet daily. We find ourselves set off by different interactions, emotions running high and hard to control. We angrily comment on a "rage-farming" post (clickbait designed to provoke outrage), lose our temper with the people around us, or even lose our sense of all social contracts and decorum, behaving in ways that seem slightly mad.

(Or completely unhinged.)

At work we speed up the release of projects, jumping into fixing before we've really understood what to fix. We set arbitrary deadlines for production, insisting that things be completed by the deadline when things don't need that kind of pressure (after all, in most professions, no one is going to die if a deadline is missed). We have back-to-back meetings to endlessly discuss, eat lunch at our desks, or cram in a few loads of laundry if we're working from home. We try to rely on doing things the way they've always been done, following the old systems.

We keep speeding up, hoping to catch up and connect back into what used to be, and it's just ... not ... working.

Compartmentalization can kill your life

Compartmentalization can kill your life,
siloed and solo, small container
pressure cookers of all by yourself
mountains mounting not talking and
though sometimes safe, they
eventually wall fall all on you
crushing, cursing and chambers of the
heart are apart, but connected beating—
so are our lives and trying to pretend
we are islands, alone, is to entirely
disregard the stream, consciousness
where we reside, currently currented and
we need more connection, not less and
though those barriers used to bear us
from work to life and back, we're not
there where we were anymore and
now then before now, now, now
we melt
mergemeld and
there is no professional
no personal lives lived,
it's all one
one live
living
life.

How many times in the past have you heard someone say, "What happens in/at _____ stays in/at _____?" Whether it's Vegas, home, or work, there's a sense of maintaining strict control of sharing information about what occurs in one place versus another. Naturally we don't necessarily want to share everything about everything in every instance (I'm not suggesting we abandon all discretion), but this idea of never sharing anything personal (or drastically limiting what we share) in a professional context or vice versa has been left in the dust of technology. Once we had mobile phones, video calls, and global social media, the illusion of separation quickly came to a screeching halt.

The problem is compartmentalization often masquerades as a superpower.

Whether you're the master of multitasking, or the virtuoso of separation, this kind of rigidity sometimes seems like an easier path to take rather than deal with the messiness (temporary, btw) of merging. Work stays at work, personal stuff stays at home, and life is all sunshine and rainbows. There are a number of clients I know whose work lives are towers of efficiency, but whose personal lives are like forgotten attics, full of dusty boxes labeled "emotions" and "personal relationships." When you're compartmentalizing this way, you run the risk of forgetting about entire sections of your life and, more importantly, about yourself. Picture this: you're juggling a demanding job, family responsibilities, and a social life. Each of these areas of your life is neatly sectioned off, but guess what? Stress doesn't care about your color-coded calendar. Studies show that chronic stress can wreak havoc on your health, from insomnia and headaches to more serious issues such as cardiovascular problems.

Compartmentalization might seem like a shield, but it's more like a grenade with a pulled pin, just waiting for you to lose your grip.

Compartmentalization doesn't play nice with relationships, either personal or business. Picture a couple, each with their own separate worlds. He's got his career, she's got hers, and their personal connection? It's like a neglected garden. Without open communication and shared experiences, relationships wither. Trust erodes, intimacy fades, and before you know it, you're living with a stranger. Compartmentalization turns partners into cohabitants, sharing a space but not a life. At work, different departments in a company become like islands, each working independently with little communication or collaboration. It might seem like a streamlined approach, but it's a breeding ground for inefficiency and missed opportunities.

The danger of compartmentalization is that it creates a façade of success while silently eroding the foundation of well-being.

Case in Point

I once worked with a queen of compartmentalization (I'll call her Mary) and you probably know someone like her, too. On the surface, she had it all together—a successful career, a picturesque family, and a social calendar that would make anyone jealous. But dig a little deeper, and there was a woman stretched thin, emotionally exhausted from keeping her work and personal life in separate zip codes. Mary's health took a hit, both mentally and physically. She had bags under her eyes, stress-induced migraines, and a sense of emptiness that even her packed schedule couldn't fill. She was very nearly burnt out, using all her mental and emotional energy to keep things tightly wound, and she'd lost herself, and what she really needed and wanted in the process.

Frankly, there are too many Marys (and Mikes and Morgans, for that matter) running around, leading our world. Outwardly successful, inwardly miserable. They look great, but it's tough to make good decisions when you're unhappy, tired, and stressed. Now, I'm not suggesting that compartmentalization isn't a useful tool from time to time, but using it as a day-to-day operating system goes against everything humans were designed for and the effects are showing. Unfortunately, many of us have bought into the idea that material success will bring us the happiness we want, but at least half the people I know who are successful in this way are unhappy.

Compartmentalization is literally killing us. We can't go on pretending we're separate.

BUT…

Ego gets in the way

Ego gets in the way
of so many small things
and all the big things
when it comes to being real
being really connected
and really really present,
Shreklike working, ogre layers
need peeling like onions and we
just have to find ourselves in the
reflections of one another and
let
it
all
go,
problems, prestige, politics, and
all the foolish earthly things,
earthy garden soil, and
strip back, step back, and see
in each other
humanity, true,
and start,
from one small point to
build connections
to ourselves
to each other
and stop worrying about
how we look
to others but worry more
about how we sleep at night—
who are we really when nobody is looking?
Ego gets in the way, fights, sneaky
bravado bullying its way into the faces
of the ones we think we can overpower

when we don't feel seen or heard or valued
our egos egg us on to louder and louder
brash statements and bold, creating pushback
waves of resistance slamming us on the
shores of the land we hoped to touch
touch down.
We can't ego our way into anything,
false self,
unfounded,
only out, outward facing, and
antagony antagonizing us and them and all, so
drop it if you can, strong underneath and see
what happens next if you
remove your ego
from the equation.
Equalize.

Our egos don't want to let go of the idea of perfection, of measuring up to an external metric of success. When we're all up in our ego, we're not really able to sit with the truth of what it is we really want and need. We get competitive, start heading down the zero-sum thinking path of win–lose, building those walls instead of bridges. This egoic desire digs in, undermining our ability to connect and collaborate. We just want to be the best, the brightest, the first. We get highly focused on ourselves and what we think we should want. Our ego doesn't want us to be open about our struggles, fears, and shortcomings, or risk being perceived as weak or incapable. It stands firmly in the way of our vulnerability and keeps us scared of truly connecting.

We need to let ourselves and others off the hook of inhuman standards.

We need to be able to let the ego go,

BUT…

We Fear Letting Go

People are afraid to let go of their carefully constructed façades, even though these façades are just another set of walls. Whether it's a desire to be seen as a superhero of sorts, with a polished and perfect exterior, presenting ourselves to the world as the ultimate version of who we think we should be, or fear of judgment, and the extreme pressures of social expectations and comparison culture can crush people's desires to be real very quickly.

When façadewalls fail

When façadewalls fail,
fall, fell flat,
it all falls, our masks made
for happy-faced productions
producing products perfectly and
pretending the world's not on fire
white knighting it out, knuckled down,
knocking in, knocking on, doors of
our own being and what we've made,
armor to survive the daily cruelty of
factory-made schedules trying to fit
knowledge-based economies of scale
and we are forced to show up false to
keep the balls in the air, juggling and
you can see the cracks, can't you?

Unfortunately, façades like these rest on pretty shaky ground, rarely constructed from an internal sense of self and when they fail, everything comes tumbling down. Divorce, job loss, addiction, burnout, and many more terrible life consequences rush in to fill the void that was hidden behind the fakery and we lose ground both personally and professionally. Not only that, but people have been punished for being very real, sharing too much or being too vulnerable in the past.

In a professional landscape that frequently prioritizes appearances and conformity, being too real can be a risky venture.

While nothing beats genuine self-expression for fostering trust and camaraderie, getting into the TMI (too much information) zone on your personal or professional details and challenges might lead to unintended consequences.

Again, don't just take my word for it...

- A 2018 study by Gibson, Harari, and Marr, published for the American Psychological Association found that, across three laboratory studies, disclosures of weakness made by a higher (versus peer) status co-worker negatively affected the receiver's perception of the discloser's status and consequently undermined the discloser's influence, encouraged task conflict, and led to lower relationship quality with the discloser.[8]
- In 2017, an employee at a major tech company posted an anonymous, heartfelt blog on The Guardian website about his struggles with mental health and the company's lack of support. Instead of receiving empathy, he faced backlash from colleagues and superiors, ultimately leading to his dismissal. This case highlights the harsh consequences of being too open about personal challenges, even when advocating for positive change.[9]

What's worse is that the penalties for authenticity are not distributed equally.

Women, in particular, often face additional challenges when it comes to being candid in the workplace. A 2020 study published in the *Frontiers of Psychology* found that women expressing anger at work are more likely to face backlash compared to their male counterparts.[10] This is especially challenging when we're trying to identify and solve real interpersonal problems on both the small and large scales. Not only that, but we've also been pushed to "be positive" (why don't you smile more?), which blinds us to uncovering and acknowledging real problems.

Workplaces claim to value authenticity, but the reality reflects a bias toward positivity.

This bias is fueled by pop psychology and studies on specific things that get extrapolated and grabbed by the media and repeated so often they become accepted fact.* A Stanford study in 2018 exploded across the media with headlines such as "a positive attitude literally makes your brain work better" and "the secret to happiness is all in your head."[11] Spoiler alert: it was a study following elementary school kids that measured how well they did in math relative to their attitudes about math. Not exactly widely applicable and trying to find a link to the actual study was a lengthy process.

Unfortunately, this kind of pop psychology sticks. Employees who consistently exude positivity are perceived as better team players, even if it means they're suppressing authentic emotions. Pressure to maintain a cheerful facade at all costs can stifle genuine self-expression and contributes to the mental and emotional labor expected from employees in a "happy" workplace. It's also completely unrealistic. While it's nice to maintain a positive outlook most of the time, it's not effective for assessing a life, a job, or problems in most spheres. Toxic positivity anyone?

---

* This is a personal pet peeve of mine—see my note back in Chapter 2 about "imposter syndrome," grr.

We Like to Be Comfortable

Change is an uncomfortable, painful place. We like to inhabit our habits and not stray too far from the well-known paths. Confrontation of long-held beliefs and clinging to the ways things have been done before isn't an easy process. I once had a conversation with a therapist who estimated from her experience that only 25 percent or so of the population is doing therapeutic work to improve their understanding of themselves and others. Increasing your social and emotional intelligence can be a long and difficult journey, especially if you had trauma as a kid or in your early adult years and need to spend some time unpacking your personal baggage. It often involves tears, feeling all the feels, experiencing setbacks and pain. No wonder people are reluctant. Not only that, it can also feel a bit Sisyphian† to try to change the ways things are done, always uncovering new layers of things to change.

We're Stuck With Some Outdated Standards and Beliefs

It can sometimes seem like things are never going to change, particularly when we witness huge backlash to new ideas. Just witness the recent push against diversity, equity, and inclusion (DEI), despite numerous studies showing we win in life and business when we have different kinds of people and thinkers around our tables. According to a recent study by Pew Research, more than half of survey respondents felt that focusing on DEI was a good thing, but those who retain power in our current framework are madly fighting to hold the line of the status quo.[12] I bet you can easily guess who they are...

Yup. Shocker. In 2023...

---

† For those of you not familiar with good old Sisyphus, he's the devious, murderous tyrant who was punished by the gods in Greek mythology for his crimes by having to constantly roll a rock uphill, only to have it roll back down every time he neared the top. Eternal damnation, indeed!

The survey respondents most likely to view DEI negatively were white men over the age of 50 and who vote conservatively.[‡]

Don't believe me? Just look around.

- We think competitively, not collaboratively.
- We think we have to grind and hustle to be successful.
- We let workaholism be an acceptable and rewarded addiction.
- We pay leaders waaaaay more than the people they lead.
- We equate material success with smarts.
- We don't invest in the things that actually improve our outcomes as a society (witness the pouring of cash into military endeavors while education and health care starve).

Our outdated standards and beliefs are hurting us.

We Have to Think About the "Big O" Too

Big O! Operating systems, my friend (I know, you went naughty there for a moment, but come back). We live in systems, interconnected through the world. We laugh at the "butterfly effect" in time travel science fiction, but in reality, our actions here do affect others across the world. On a small scale, our home systems of family, friends, community, and work keep us grounded and safe (for the most part). On a large scale, our systems of governance at the local, federal, and international levels help

---

[‡] Now, I don't want to diss them too hard here, so don't #notallmen me on this. We know it's not all of them, but there are enough roadblockers to make changing things slow. Honestly, I feel for them. It can be discombobulating when the subterranean structure underneath all of your existing beliefs begins to quake. And it's not just the men. Anyone who has been successful in the past system (including those who had to act like men to fit in), compartmentalizing away, hiding behind their facade, gaining success by dutifully playing the game is likelier than not to vigorously resist this shift. It goes back to enjoying comfort—we don't always want to get off the couch and think about how the world could be if it benefited everyone, not just a select few. Our actions show that we don't value what we say we value.

provide guardrails on society. In business, everything we do and provide works in a system and it's pretty clear that our systems are broken, for many of us. Some of us, with that old "'survival of the fittest" mentality may see that everything is fine, but with all that's going on in the world, it's becoming clearer that it's everyone's job to work toward something better for everyone, not just what we've deemed "fittest."

We don't live in an "either/or" world, we live in an "and" world.

The world is not binary, mutually exclusive, or separate, and, personally, I like to dream of a world where people show up entirely as who they are and we manage to understand and accept and love them just as they are and just where they're at. I'd like to see a world where everyone's needs are met and where we are all living within our means, not consuming at the cost of someone else's misery. Now that we're in the information age, and particularly with the rise of artificial intelligence (AI), we need to lean fully into our humanity, casting off the mechanized ideas of strict working hours, precision execution, and set processes. When we measure, we need to look at both productivity and the people who produce, by bringing in new measurements and working in new ways, but we can't get there with the same old style of leadership.

We Can't Rely on Power Anymore

"With great power comes great responsibility." You may have heard this phrase popularized recently in the Marvel Spider-Man franchise as Uncle Ben says it to Peter Parker. The phrase was borrowed from Voltaire, the famed French author, but the concept of power and responsibility walking hand in hand goes back as far as the legend of the sword of Damocles. As the story goes, the courtier Damocles was happy to trade places with the ruling tyrant of the time, but was dismayed to find that a sword was suspended by a single horsehair over the throne as a constant reminder of the worry associated with governance. A single bad decision can have far-reaching impacts. As business leaders, we may not have the same kind of great power that comes along with high-level political leadership, but the more we gain influence and control in our business structures, the more people we employ and care for and the more impact we generate, the more our obligation grows to take responsibility for the power structures we're maintaining or creating. This includes choosing metrics for success that take our collective humanity into account and not just the money. Depending on where you're situated in your company, you will either have control or influence over what is being measured. A persuasive case for adding more humane metrics into our pool of measurement goes a long way and the things we measure in business can and do influence the things we measure in the wider world.

We often hear critiques of society, but we don't necessarily associate those critiques with our own leadership.

Society isn't a thing

Society isn't a thing
we carry outside of us.
It's carried within us
and
business within it,
and no one else but us
is responsible for changing
all the things we don't like.

One of the big walls is how we choose our leaders. It's the main way we affect how we'll be governed, managed, and led, in business, in politics, or in other relationships.

Ideally, we'd make this choice very carefully and thoughtfully, gauging our choices against our own values and how the people conduct themselves according to those values. If you were joining a company, you'd do your due diligence to understand the leadership philosophy and examine their workplace practices to see if their values align with yours. Unfortunately, many of us are not as politically educated or informed as we could be, or just don't have time to do the reading on the candidates and companies we choose. In addition, people who want to be leaders carefully curate what we see and don't see. Have you noticed lately that we allow people to get into positions of power and then start finding things out about them that we don't like? We choose based on our impressions, and our impressions are vague at best and completely wrong at worst. As a result, many of our leaders are not real with themselves or us. They are disconnected, misguided, and doing things that the citizens and employees they govern and manage actively oppose. We are choosing people and seeing leaders who take an individual, self-focused approach to leadership, rather than leaders who consider the people in their care and what's best for them. The good news is that mid-career or early-stage leaders have a lot of runway to exercise their power differently, and the changes we make on a local level or company level can influence change at higher levels too. If we want a society that shows more care for everyone involved, we need to call in leaders who don't seem to care for others and divest ourselves from them if they are unable or unwilling to change.

We Need Responsible Stewards

I was sitting at a table with a highly educated and experienced group of women, and we got into a relatively heated political discussion about the state of leadership in business and in the world, and, in the end, we agreed that what we needed were more leaders who understood the direct relationship between wealth and power and responsibility. We know that wealth grants power in this world, but we also know that, according to recent research, as people gain wealth, they risk of losing their empathy for others.[13] If they are insulated from the world's issues by their wealth and power, they may have a stronger sense of independence and freedom from others, which might make them less likely to care responsibly for the power that they wield and less likely to care for the people who help to drive their wealth. This means that we need more leaders who are acutely conscious of the disparity and who actively work to maintain their levels of empathy and connection to others. Leaders who care in this way could be our new responsible stewards. We need to foster more of this idea of stewardship, the job of taking care of or supervising something. This divorces the person from the power and wealth, framing power and wealth as something that requires care and then is passed on, not something that is sought for its own end and clung to fiercely. With more power comes more responsibility and we need more people in power who know themselves well, who care for others and who are willing to show us who they really are in order for us to develop the trust we need in them to be responsible stewards.

What does good stewardship look like?

Why Ani DiFranco had it right

Why Ani DiFranco had it right
when keeping her business great
instead of big was
she kept her heart
and head firmly planted in the individual
and collective nature of the city where
she lived and on the businesses who lived
there with her and called them in when
she needed help, supporting them when
they faltered too, reciprocal and in
right relationship with them meant that she
and they
could thrive together, not one elevated more
over another and stayed away from the pure
profit machines that hoover up workers and
spit out cash and broken people, exploitative and
she
refused
to grow
at the expense of others who helped and that,
that is what is right.
We can't continue to endlessly grow,
we aren't infinite and if we don't
whole self it out, we'll break into
a million billion pieces along with the
planetary, destruction imminent,
countdown underway, and Ani,
she had it right and
we
can
too.

Here's what responsible stewardship could look like:

Caring for your people in more ways than a paycheck can handle:

Aside from direct remuneration, we need direct communication about the issues our teams face that may inhibit their performance at work and finding ways to adjust. For example, it may mean offering flexible hours to parents or unlimited personal time off so employees can take time to do the things outside of work that increase their well-being and make them better employees. We might also look at resourcing our teams in different ways to ensure that we don't have one person expected to do the jobs of three people with the resources of one. This means a bit more digging into job descriptions and tasks, but the time spent on making work workable for more of our people is time well spent.

Choosing different ways to reinvest in the business:

We often send profit to executive pay or to shareholder value, but we could cut back a bit on those and reinvest a chunk of our profit into the people who make the business run. Spending on livable wages, offering career growth opportunities, investing in profit sharing with the employees or beefing up benefits are all ways to take the profit that is generated by the people in the company and let them share more fairly in the fruits of their labor.

Listening more carefully to those who are at different levels

In a number of my clients' companies, it was apparent that the executive team was not getting the full picture of what employees at frontline levels were experiencing and were therefore unable to make the big-picture adjustments that would actually alleviate the stress that teams were under. They also weren't hearing messages about the level of intensity that employees were experiencing if the company had a philosophy of focusing on performance above all else, so there were high levels of burnout and churn that were costing hundreds of thousands of dollars. They also weren't able to foster enough trust for employees to fully disclose any issues, so things were getting missed.

Going for reasonable rather than rigid:

Often, the companies that weren't doing the above things also made their timelines, deliverables, and goals unreachable, setting up a climate of failure and stress. When they adjusted for their actual resources and put in reasonable timelines for projects and reasonable projections for growth, running the business in a way that took into account the full lives of the people who are in it, their performance paradoxically improved. This one simple thing made space for different perspectives, for time off to do other things besides work and it deeply embraced the individual within the collective, celebrating the achievements of what we can do when we really work well together.

Honoring the cycles of productivity, rest, and reflection.

In her book, *Do Less*,[14] Kate Northrup talks about how we don't rest in our current world—everything else in nature rests and grows in different seasons, so why don't we pay more attention to the cycles of projects and plans and our own growth? She's written the book for women, but it applies to all of us. Responsible stewards know their charges and honor them in their natural forms and people are creatures of nature. We need our seasons too.

May I speak plainly?

- *No one's coming to rescue us. It's us.*
- *If we want better leaders, we have to make better choices.*
- *If we want to **BE** better leaders, we have to **BE** the better choice.*

We need to be in right relationship.

With ourselves.

With others.

With the world.

We are more connected than ever. We need leaders who understand this and can guide us from a place of responsible stewardship. We need to look at things differently. As we start to open up to embracing difference versus fitting in, looking to what's next for leadership and business, as well as calling in responsible stewards, one of the key things we need are people who are willing to see, discuss, and take down the walls that get in our way, by looking at things differently.

If we're going to be different, we need to look for different measures of success.

CHAPTER 4

What Are We Measuring?

The prize is not the prize anymore.

People have historically been commodified as "resources" or "capital" and were encouraged and happy to work for external rewards—a big salary, a corner office, a fancy title, and more. But what happens to our business lives when the prize isn't the prize anymore? People aren't interested in titles or promotions when it means heavier responsibilities, being expected to do more with less or making work the priority over life. Businesses are now grappling with the reality that people don't want to work themselves to the bone for shareholder value. They want to work at a different pace and make meaningful contributions while preserving their mental health and well-being. They want to work remotely or in a hybrid form because it shortens commutes and is a better use of their time and energy. They want to have room for physical activity, for social activity, and for their families and friends in different ways. Back in previous eras where the work schedule of an executive was manageable because their spouse took on all the household labor, people were happy to work for the title and long hours. But now that gender roles have become less defined, women are often primary breadwinners and household labor is becoming more evenly split, people aren't as interested in the same carrots and are not as intimidated by the same sticks. The prize is not the prize anymore.

People are motivated by more than money these days and are seeking ways to make a strong contribution to their workplaces, not just collect a paycheck.

Now that people don't want to work the way we used to work, we are looking at people and valuing them for the complete humanity they can bring to the business world, instead of for just the tasks they perform.

This shift has been driven largely by the younger generations raising the question of "why" we work, tying work to personal fulfillment far more than the previous generations did. The pandemic only accelerated this shift, causing a huge percentage of us to consider the value of the work we do and our own value within it. People aren't willing anymore to take a job for the sake of paying the bills. They want to enjoy their work, enjoy the people they work with, and still have time and flexibility left over for living their lives.

They want different kinds of work and different ways of doing it. Businesses need to adapt their measures accordingly.

What are we measuring

What are we measuring
these days, in business?
Numbersnumbersnumbers,
revenue growth, and endless profit
hungry for marketshare power,
short-term gains for shareholder wins,
turnover churn, and endless stream of
bodies moving through rules roles and
chalking it all up to
no one wants to work anymore when
it's just that no one wants to work
for you, for the conditions you set for
the sandbox shape and expecting
all of "them" to fit without ever considering
the difference in how people are
and how they work and allowing for
all the humanity long-term looking to
the horizon of longevity.
We are measuring all the
wrong things, money matters,
of course, but so does
meaning, mental health,
activity and rest, and all the
dancing things, reciprocal, and
businesses that balance both
might not be spectacular in growth
but sustainability? Five stars.
Grow slowly, grow well, measure the
right things and find the right people.
When we only settle for money metrics
we're missing out on how the world has
changed and, on fire, we'd better change
quickly, and pick up the pieces, relational
and find your place in the grand scheme

scheduled, and stretch elastic into
what's beyond what we have now and
stop. doing. all. the. same. things.
that. haven't. worked. aren't working, won't.
Measure
differently.
For real.

We really need to think about what we're measuring these days, not only what counts as good leadership and why but also what metrics we're using for the people who power our organizations.

We know that measurement is a fundamental component of business. We can't improve the state of performance if we don't measure. When we were living in an industrial age and every bolt had to be in the same place, the same way at the same time to make the machine go, it made sense that we would compartmentalize, streamline, disconnect, and behave in machine-like ways, as if we were all cogs and gears. Our key performance indicators were equally compartmentalized, measuring only in dollars: bottom lines, profit, revenue, cashflow, savings, and stock prices. Sure, we might take a nod to culture and try to measure employee engagement and satisfaction, but the dollar still held sway and caused us to always drive our people harder, to do more with less. In some places, this has driven working conditions back into the pre-union days of the 1920s, or worse, where companies are treating employees more like machines than as living, breathing people.

Case in Point

In 2021, thanks to some hard investigation by the New York Times, *inhumane stories started coming out of Amazon. From messing up the leave system so badly that many employees were shortchanged hundreds of dollars per cheque[15] or fired even though they were on leave, and not paid back until months later, to exposing horrifying working conditions in warehouses and for delivery drivers, Amazon is a classic example of a company that clearly values profit over people. Many of the most contentious policies go back to the founder's original policy of finding efficiencies, such as deliberately encouraging churn to keep productivity high and wages low.[16] There are other well-known public examples, from Walmart employees on food stamps[17] and many private examples from my own practice of managers and executives in large companies expected to pick up the work of as many as two or three employees when people are laid off and not replaced. People are being driven like machines and expected to perform at an inhuman level to drive efficiency.*

Human capital is

Human capital is
a sickening phrase,
reducing us to
numbers on a page.
Enraged, staged,
dehumanized, and
unforgiving.
A relic of gold,
industrializing,
mechanizing the soul
and disguising our
inner resources
as external, traded
for wages beyond
expectations undermined,
signed on the dotted line,
and we the people
refuse to be
machined
anymore.

What Is Performance?

For many years, we've only been looking at business performance in terms of what gets done to drive economic success and satisfy shareholders and profit margins. We maintain an intense focus on execution of tasks and the achievement of objectives. It's all about the measurable results, the objectives, key performance indicators, metrics, and return on investment.

We talk a good game about vision, mission, values, but let's get real about why we're here in business.

We speak to businesses doing good in the world, about providing resources and helping people get what they need. We think about being fulfilled in our work. All of these things are true, businesses do help our world go around. Sometimes this talk of vision even helps us get through our days when we feel ground down by the relentless speed of checking off objectives on endless project plans. But, the reality is we all have bills to pay and so we work.

We've been in it for the money.

Unless you're already independently wealthy and living off the interest on your investments, at least part of your reason for your work is to get money. Now, money in and of itself is a reasonable marker for business performance, and necessary for paying the bills, but as a measurement in business or life, money is a way of keeping score, of seeking a tangible result.

(Which is kind of hilarious because money is a representation of reality, just a fantasy we've all agreed to buy into, literally, but that's another book entirely.)

You need a bottom line to

You need a bottom line to
run the business, it's not
business without one but
what's on the bottom line
is entirely open for discussion,
and newsflash,
it's not only moneynumberstime,
but love on the bottom line,
bottoming out,
humanity human, and
it's not a yesno binary but
(like all other things)
an "and world" of yes, and
what else?
Titles, sure,
cash, sure
promotions, sure but
what about us?
Our families, our
lives outside, the
other things we all need, and want
to do that are shovedstrangled down
let's put the rest to rest,
on a line, that's fine
bottom…
from the bottom
of our hearts,
breathing room,
some slow space to work
and realize
not everything needs to be done right now
not everything needs to grow apace
and we,
as humans,

are not business nor
busybees, but
building
better so
foundationally, we need
to consider, reconsider, rise,
and include more on the bottom line
than money.

Whether it's measured in stock prices, churn rates, profit margins, or bonuses, it's about the money. Businesses don't survive without measuring. We've gotten very good at keeping our eye on the prize as leaders, BUT…

What do we do when the prize is not the prize anymore?

As companies try to motivate different generations of workers, they keep dangling these old school carrots, but employees are walking away. They are looking for more flexibility in their schedules, more control over their earnings, more fulfillment in their work, and freedom from the politics of the office environment.

Don't just take my word for it:

According to a report from the *Wall Street Journal* in 2021:[18]

- The number of self-employed workers has risen to its highest level in 11 years.
- The share of U.S. workers employed by a company of 1,000 employees or more has fallen for the first time since 2004.
- In September 2021, workers resigned from 4.4 million jobs.
- About 22 out of 52 economists surveyed said that workplace participation would never return to pre pandemic levels.

I can't tell you the number of leaders I talk to who are stretched thin, expected to do the work of three people with the resources of one, work more hours, make more sacrifices of their personal lives to bow down to the almighty bottom line and sure, we need a bottom line in business, but we don't need to make revenue the only thing that matters in business.

Money cannot be the only marker of performance any more.

The health of business is dependent on the health of people that run it.

We need to get real about our capacity, what is right for us as humans.

People, including us, are not robots. We are not "resources" or "capital." We are not cogs in a well-oiled machine. We are not replaceable. We might have to take a little more time to find out where exactly we belong, but we are unique and each of us has a place. As leaders, we can find our own place and help others find theirs.

We're moving out of the industrial, mechanical age and we need to adapt.

For the past hundred years or so, we needed people who could perform like robots, putting the same bolt in the same place, at the same time in the same way, every time. We modeled our business practices on the way machines operated, smooth processes leading to the same product every time. We leaned hard into mechanizing tasks, systemizing things, mining resources, and growing, growing, growing. We loved the speed, the efficiency, the pace of growth, and the seemingly endless vistas of opportunity. This has been a wild, exciting ride, with so much to be celebrated, and it's been fun, but we're hitting the limits of what our planet can handle and the limits of our capacity to act like machines. (Just think for a minute about your calendar, packed with back-to-back meetings, no time to eat, pee, or breathe).

The endless industrial growth party is over.
Different leadership is needed now.
If we want to stay in business, we need to measure performance in different, more sustainable ways.

Good measurement means leaning *into* humanity not out.

It means being whole as people and seeing the whole picture as we measure, but there's a catch.

We can move from a place of completeness and connection instead of compartmentalization and disconnection, but we can't do that at the current pace. We have to consider letting our foot off the gas, to move away from endless growth. Even the economists are getting on board, exemplified by Kate Raworth and her "Donut" theory of economics.[19] This theory speaks to how we live in a finite system and we are finite beings, so infinite growth doesn't work. When we're looking at measurement, we need to accept that businesses are finite too and we need to start pulling back just a little, to get deeper into handling all moving pieces that go into connecting fully with one another. This means taking more time to connect, not less. We're not suggesting that things will get less efficient, only that they'll get more focused and more human.

We have to slow down, relax a little.

Go a little slower to get better results

Go a little slower to get better results
take your time and scope
out all the possible peoplewaysthings we
can use to use our skillstalentsbrains
to very best advantage,
this person here, that one there and
switch, switch it up from time to time and
dancing around, everyone slots into the pegspuzzled
right way up and round, squaring off on
the problem, not on each other and
when we take our time,
we get there faster.

Okay, I can hear your inner voices now… "Lazaruk, I can barely go to the bathroom between meetings, how the f&%$ am I supposed to slow down?" Don't worry, we'll get to that, but here's the outline:

We need to lean into taking our time—metaphorically, literally, socially.

I want to acknowledge that some people enjoy running like race cars and feel their best when they're highly productive, which is okay as long as they're happy. I also estimate from the thousands of conversations I've had over the past 15 years of consulting that fully half of the high-powered, outwardly successful people who run like this aren't running for the joy of it. They're living in Formula One land because our society has attached so much of our worth to our work and they feel unworthy when they aren't racing. They're workaholics. They're afraid. They're tired. They're worried about what will happen to them at work if they choose to slow down and take more control over their schedules. More importantly, they're realizing that their addiction to work is impacting their lives, but are finding it hard to cut back because workaholism is the most rewarded and socially acceptable addiction in our society today. They have been willing to sacrifice their health, their relationships, and their well-being for the sake of the rewards, but even then, they're beginning to realize it's not sustainable or rewarding in the long run.

Workaholism and its rewards are not the only reason we're caught in the speed cycle. I also want to acknowledge that we're all running this race of back-to-back meetings and long hours because some people who run the businesses in which we work want to squeeze as much productivity out of us as they can. They want us to run, but it hurts.

Don't just take my word for it, here's some information from the Centers for Disease Control and Prevention (CDC):[20]

- Workers who report stressors such as high job strain (high demands, with low levels of decision-making power) have an increased frequency of heart disease [Theorell et al. 2016].

- Role overload can lead to decreased job and family satisfaction, lower organizational commitment, and higher absenteeism [Duxbury et al. 2008].
- Having control over one's work (how, where, and when people work) is beneficial for work–family balance and worker well-being [Kelly and Moen 2007].

Companies have decided that it's more valuable for us to keep running than it is for us to slow down, but the tide is turning and we are starting to see the benefits of slowing down.

We decide what is valuable in our world, so there's no reason why we can't decide that speed isn't the only factor in getting from Point A to Point B.

When we speed, we miss the details of certain people being excluded, of voices being missed at the table and we risk coming up with solutions that are merely band-aids on the wounds of our world. We end up outwardly materially successful, but inwardly miserable. The world seems to be coming apart at the seams with the reckless pace of growth we've adopted, and it would be good to make some repairs while we still have time.

It's all arbitrary

It's all arbitrary,
so if we get to make it up,
why don't we make it easier and more pleasing
instead of harder?

We all know that there can be great satisfaction in setting clear goals, prioritizing and striving for excellence. It can feel good to be a leader and increase your influence. I'm all for taking clear steps on a purposeful path, but we really have to question where those paths lead. Instead of blindly pursuing a new pay grade or a title, we're questioning why and how we're working. Now more than ever, we're getting to choose.

For this new paradigm, we need to rewrite our standards of performance, to measure differently, in a more human way. We need to consider how the whole person fits into the modern workplace and how the modern workplace fits the whole person. We also need to consider what success looks like for us individually and collectively and to reduce the comparison between us.

Systems thinking teaches

Systems thinking teaches
that everything connects to
everything and
there just isn't much point in
pretending
that we are separate and
siloed and
I get that people want to specialize for
seeming efficiency and depth but
seriously, we just can't expect to pretend
that we're an assembly line, factoried
eight-hour days and weekends when
our world is melding, melting, and we
need to connect to each other to find out
what the left right hand is doing so
we aren't repeating, stuck in useless
doing of the same doings that everyone
else has done for all the donuts and coffee
over all the years in break rooms and board rooms
and repeating the same things
expecting different results
is insanity.
Let's just stop
pretending
that all this disconnection works
when we know
it doesn't.
Seriously,
how can we
all get along
if we don't
dare to
connect, talk, feel?

We Need to Humanize

A huge part of this shift is having us lean into being human and that means really talking with one another, trusting each other, and feeling our feelings. I know that's not usually where business books go, but truly, emotional regulation and handling ourselves well under stress is the new superpower. In particular, the need to humanize is made even greater by the speedy rise of AI. AI is poised to take over a number of different kinds of jobs in the next 7 to 10 years and we will need to ensure that we take advantage of the opportunity to hold on to the work that only humans can do.

Don't take my word for it though:

According to McKinsey Global's 2023 report on Generative AI and the Future of Work:[21]

- By 2030, activities that account for up to 30 percent of hours currently worked across the U.S. economy could be automated.
- More than half of the ~8.6 million recent occupational shifts in the United States involved workers leaving roles in food services, customer service, office support, and production.
- Demand for clerks could decrease by 1.6 million jobs, in addition to losses of 830,000 for retail salespersons, 710,000 for administrative assistants, and 630,000 for cashiers.

Anything repetitive can be automated and now that AI is generative, meaning it can learn from huge datasets and create new content, the pace of this change will only accelerate.

We have machines to handle the machinable business.

We have the opportunity to humanize the rest.

We need to get real, and that means leaning into our collective messiness and uniqueness and difficulty. Sounds daunting, I know, but stay with me here. If you're not into getting real for the joy of being human or the joy of being a better leader, here's the business case.

Paradoxically, humanizing business leads to better business outcomes.

It might take more time and be tricky to navigate, but it does. It drives real connection and real connection drives engagement. Engagement leads to happier teams and happier teams mean better business.

Seriously… don't just take my word for it:

- According to a Gallup survey, highly engaged employees are 21 percent more productive than their disengaged counterparts. Job satisfaction, as a crucial component of happiness, leads to improved performance and increased motivation.[22]
- Research by the Center for American Progress estimates that the cost of replacing an employee can be up to 21 percent of their annual salary.[23]
- A 2013 Gallup study that appeared in the *Harvard Business Review* demonstrates a strong correlation between employee engagement and profitability. Companies with highly engaged employees experience 21 percent higher profitability.[24]
- Research by the University of Warwick found that happy employees are up to 12 percent more productive, indicating a strong connection between well-being and business success.[25]

Case in Point

Costco, a company consistently recognized for its happy employees, is also highly profitable. It offers competitive wages, excellent benefits, and opportunities for advancement, resulting in a motivated work-force that contributes to the company's financial success. Costco's stock performance and financial results reflect the benefits of investing in employee happiness.[26]

Some companies still don't get it. They insist that productivity and revenue are the only measures of success.

You know the ones, those who push their employees past physical endurance or pay them so little they're on food stamps or deny them leave when they're sick. They are inhuman. Lucky for us (and eye-opening for them), the reckoning is coming, and is already here. It's you and me, people who are getting real, increasing their self-awareness and the awareness of others around them that are pushing back on this dynamic of pushing people to the breaking point and simply replacing them. We're pushing back on packed calendars, early mornings, late nights, and forced return-to-office policies. We might not have the new way all figured out yet, but we know there is more to work than money.

We know that we need to make space for the reality of being human.

We can stop buying into the myth that money is the only thing that makes a business worth working. We can get real and lead from a more forgiving, more human place for ourselves and our teams. We can't keep acting like machines—we won't last, so how about this?

- We can measure results achieved rather than time spent achieving them.
- We can reward balanced schedules over packed calendars.
- We can create project plans that are achievable in realistic timelines.
- We can incentivize completing work in the assigned working hours.
- We can reward well-resourced projects and teams.
- We can spend more on employee health and well-being.
- We can track the overall health and wellness of our teams.
- We can reduce the costs of churn by providing workplaces worthy of long-term stays.
- We can measure our overall success in a holistic way.

Instead of dedication to shareholder's value, let's offer a dedication to deeply knowing and understanding one another so that we perform better as a team.

The money will take care of itself.

May I speak plainly?

- *This new system is relational not transactional; we need relational measures.*
- *This new system is integrated, not compartmentalized, we need integrated measures.*
- *The key to both is connection.*

We cannot create better measures for better results without being more deeply connected to the whole picture.

It's time to embrace the messiness of wholeness—to acknowledge that our personal and professional lives are interconnected threads that weave the fabric of our existence. Breaking down walls doesn't mean chaos; it means allowing the flow of energy, creativity, and connection. It's about recognizing that the sum is greater than its parts. So, whether you're navigating the business landscape or the intricacies of personal relationships, remember: walls are meant to be broken, and integration is the key to a healthier, more fulfilling life.

Things have changed.

There is no going back.

We need our whole selves* at work and in the world.

We need to BE.

---

* At this point, you're probably thinking something like this: "Okay, Lazaruk, that all sounds great, maybe a little lofty, but how on earth do you suggest I do that? Don't worry, my friend, I've got you.")

CHAPTER 5

Your Whole Self and the Three Cs

All right everybody, let's recap:

Now that we've figured out that executive presence is an outdated concept, that our world is just a little bit f*&%ed and that no one is coming to save us, we need some help with leaning into our messy humanity. And over the next few chapters, we're going to talk about exactly how to do it. It's definitely messy, so get out your comfy clothes, roll up your sleeves, and prepare to work.

Don't just read this, either.

You're going to have to spend some time applying the principles in your daily life and I recommend at least a couple of weeks, if not a month, per stage. It took you decades to get where you are if you're reading this (it's unlikely that 10-year-olds are picking this up), so you can take a few months or more to unlearn your old habits and practice picking up the ones that are going to help you and help us get real, get connected, and get out of this mess we've made.

You're going to need to bring your whole self to the table.

What does it mean to be whole?

It doesn't mean perfect,
that's for sure.
If anything, we are
perfectlyimperfect,
souls on a learning journey, and
if I were to anagram, mnemonize
the word, I'd say it means to
wonder, bring a curious mind,
a sense of wonder, a desire to
know yourself and others.
It's to be here, wholly **here**,
not past or future, but in the moment
present, gifted.
To be whole is to be **open**,
minded, momented, desiring each
new experience or
piece of information to
give you a place to grow and
a space to **lead**,
yourself and others, to
finally, shiftchange,
evolve and
settle again,
wholeness wholesome,
complete.

This is not the time to be hiding.

Your quirks, those little idiosyncrasies that make you, well, you—they're your superpowers. Think about it. The most iconic figures in history weren't known for blending in. Nope, they stood out because they embraced their quirks and let their personalities shine. Now, I'm not recommending we follow in their footsteps, as so many of them were and are super problematic.*

BUT…

they did find ways to make their quirks work and that is definitely part of bringing your whole self to the table. Don't shy away from your quirks; flaunt them like a boss. People will appreciate your realness.

Remember, it's not about perfection, it's about connection.

Embracing your imperfections, laughing at your mistakes, and showing the world that, hey, you're human, is something that helps us all feel a little less alone. Whether it's a makeup tutorial with a few bloopers or a CEO sharing a candid moment from the office, people crave humanity. They want to see the real you, not the polished, airbrushed version. It's the imperfections that make you relatable, and in turn, build connections that transcend simple interactions.

Frankly, I dream of a new kind of workplace where we are all whole. A place where if you love the traditional dress code, you do the traditional dress code. If you want to belong in a place and you want others to come along and enjoy a different kind of dress code, you invite them to have some fun with you. We all need more fun in our lives, that's a certainty, as much as death and taxes (ugh). The old paradigm was fitting in, the new paradigm is standing out and connecting from a place of individual acceptance and connection. We need to drop the mask, bring in humanity, connect, trust, and collaborate. We don't need outdated ideas and codes of behavior anymore. We've got some good leaders showing us the way and we need more of us out there.

---

* Poke: What is it about great success that makes people so weird and disconnected eventually? I mean, we already talked about the studies that show that as people get richer, they lose their empathy proportionally but come on…WTH, you weirdos?!

Jacinda Ardern and her Facebook Lives

Jacinda Ardern and her
Facebook Lives,
world's youngest head of state,
just thirty-seven, a
twenty-year overnight success
(only the second head of state to ever
give birth while in office)
showed us all a softer face,
a humanness,
a relatability,
social media-tating, meditating,
mediating on
all the difficult things,
speaking directly to
people, populous and
never shying away from
the challenges before her
yet never playing up,
and finally,
relinquishing power
when her service was
done, not clinging on like
a tiny dinosaur and
she showed
you can
lead
with
grace
and
grit always,
always,

going with the flow,
fluid and that,
is the power of the river,
receptive, and we all
need a lot
more
water.

(I think Jacinda Ardern, former prime minister of New Zealand, is going to go down in history as one of the first and best leaders of this new style. She was one of the first leaders to bring her child into the halls of government, matter of factly accepting motherhood and bringing it face front at work. I loved the way she held her ground without ever getting bombastic, just easily let go when her time of service was done and showed us all how leadership is best managed as a relay race, not a marathon. Honestly, career politicians shouldn't be allowed. But I digress…)

Time to rip off the masks, people.

Let's dig in…

The three Cs of executive being

The three Cs of
executive being,
constant, are critical,
to holding yourself tightly
yet lightly and holding others,
spacious and it starts
with you, your
character,
congruence,
choice,
one internal,
one balanced,
one external,
turning our insides out and
creating moments of
presence, presently for all those
present with, in and around us.
Character is the core, central, who you are
when nobody's looking and when nothing matters
you decide how it all goes, smack in the middle of
mirrors, mirrored and molded and
only when it matters,
it matters.
Congruence walks the line between
you and them, in out and
balancing the needs of
the center and the
needs of the rim,
sharing what you want and not
and the line you set is the line you walk,
tightrope clean
and sometimes shifting
(in context but always you)
consistent, and finally,

choice,
accepting all the details you can change and
letting go of the ones you cannot and choosing
always choosing
your environment where you're celebrated
not tolerated and so much smoke is blown up
in dervishes of self-discovery that we always must
be mindful of the three staunch things, returning
character,
congruence,
choice.

Whatever anyone is telling you or has told you, the truth is that the heart of this thing I'm calling "executive being" doesn't come from relying on authority, wealth, power, or any other external means to confer leadership. No matter how much today's consumer hustle culture would try to tell you otherwise, and though many of the historically charismatic figures we know did attain high levels of materiality, their "being" was what propelled them forward, not the other way around.

(Theoretically, at least. You can debate me later on the chicken and egg-ness of wealth enabling leadership).

Improving your being is both simpler and more challenging than you think.

It's both an internal and external state. It is achievable in the business world and the real world through embodying, embracing, and expressing these three key concepts: **character, congruence, and choice**. That's it. Three things, not seven (though each third has a few subsets), a short list, not an exhaustive one. Each piece has a place in the puzzle and nailing these three will stand you in good stead from the boardroom to the bedroom and everywhere in between.

Let's dive deeper…

Character

I grew in rings, like a tree. At the center I'm always ten, with pink glasses and braces.

—Mary Mackey, "The Dear Dance of Eros"

Our character consists of all the things that we bring with us when we're born and all the things we learned along the way, for good or ill. Like the lauded California poet said previously, we all are the same little kid at the core.

Who we are at 4 is who we are at 104.

This is the bedrock. You know that there are some things that never change about who you are and likely never will. No matter what happens in our lives, the core of our being remains largely the same as we move through life. Character is the place where all our presence rests and knowing it well is the key to putting your most authentic self in play.

Knowing all the parts of your character, the good, bad, and the ugly, helps you understand your reactions, your patterns, and your actions. This knowledge helps you predict how you'll react in certain situations and helps you maintain your cool when the unpredictable occurs. Without knowing yourself, what you want, what you like and dislike, what you value, and what you see for your future self, you can't be present on any level.

Here's what I believe about you and your character:

- Nature doesn't make mistakes.
- Whatever container you arrived in is the perfect container to do whatever you're meant to do on the planet.
- The sooner you make friends with your container, the easier your life is going to roll.

As you come to know yourself deeply, you'll be able to express yourself more authentically and connect more deeply with others. In order to do that, you need to ensure that your insides and outsides match and that leads us to the next key piece.

Congruence

We don't live in a vacuum. While it's fantastic and desirable to be fully self-expressed and whole, it's important to consider the outside world when doing something like trying to get a job, get a date, or get anything else you might desire. Even though we're trying to change it, there is a certain amount of expectation we need to navigate so we can be seen, heard, and understood.

Case in Point

I'll never forget the first time I walked into the boardroom of the first serious business consultant I worked with. I was so excited at having invested in myself and I was ready, spiral five subject Hilroy notebook in hand, glitter pen poised...

He walked into the boardroom, looked at me, left without a word and returned a few minutes later with a hardcover notebook and said, "I want you to transfer your notes from *that* (indicating my beloved spiral notebook) into *this* (indicating his Moleskin beauty) and I never want to see *that* on my table again."

I protested, extolling the virtues of the practical spiral, and how my image consulting clients loved how down to earth I was, how accessible.

He paused and said, "What kind of consultant are you again?"

I sheepishly replied, "An image consultant."

People expect things—if you want to get real and get connected in a real way, you'd better be willing to meet them at least halfway, or willing to bear the consequences of being a challenger.

Did I like that there were expectations?
No.
Did I like that someone was telling me what to do?
No.
Did I like the results?
Yes.

This is what congruence is all about. I had to find a way for me to match the expectations the world had for someone in my industry, in a way that matched me. Sure, I could have gone the matchy–matchy way of many other consultants, but that just wasn't right. I had to find a unique way to exercise my personality and character, but within the (admittedly broad) confines of what people expected an image consultant to look like. It's the same for all of us, regardless of profession.

People like it when you make sense.

For everyone, there is a set of expectations. If you're a Reiki master and show up in a three-piece tailored suit for your client's energetic healing session, you're going to raise as many eyebrows as if you showed up in a long flowing paisley robe to the board meeting of a finance company. You get to decide how much of the expectation you want to meet and for those of you who want to create new expectations, prepare to be challenged and for things to take longer. I'm not at all suggesting you have to sublimate your personality to fit in (in fact, I don't recommend it), but finding a middle ground is always a good strategy in this case.

The more you look, act, and speak like what you say you are, the more people will take you seriously and give you opportunities, assignments, and engagements you want.

BUT…

Here's the kicker…

You *get to decide* which expectations you want to meet and when and why.

As more of us show up as our whole selves, those expectations will shift. We get to decide which expectations we want to keep as a society and which ones we want to toss. This is why this last point is so important. I used to call it "control" as in controlling all the details in your immediate power, but really, it's all about choice.

Choice

While it's true that you have no direct control over other people's perception of you, since you're not a mind reader or a hypnotist, it's also true that you can exert a *stunning* amount of choice over the small details that can influence people to think certain things about you before they even know you. I'm not suggesting any kind of "fake it 'til you make it" (which I abhor), but making sure that you've taken care of your end of the social contract in a way that makes both you and the people around you comfortable.

You get to choose what you want to change.

Case in Point

Several years ago, I worked with a young real estate agent in his early 20s. He was determined to work in high-end real estate (and in Vancouver, that's saying something) and wanted to have it all, right away, the fancy suits, the luxury car, the expensive shoes, and so on. Unfortunately, he didn't have the experience yet to suggest that his recommendations would be anything more than flashy fluff and the truth is that most people can smell bullsh&# a mile away, especially when it comes to things that just don't match. This is also how young professionals go into debt way too early and for no reason.

After a long and rather heated discussion, we agreed he'd be better off in a well-fitted made to measure suit, a mid-range luxury car with a reasonable lease and lower end details. We also talked about how his choices over details like this could expand as he expanded. I'm pleased to say he earned his way into the high-end properties within two years—he made conscious choices not only about his appearance, but also checked his behavior. He worked hard, he learned a lot, and controlled for his age by shadowing more experienced team members until he grasped the ins and outs of his profession and he lost the entitled attitude that was holding him back.

Here are just a few things that people will judge about you as they meet and work with you:

- Intelligence
- Level of education
- Socioeconomic status
- Desirability/Dateability
- Competence

Turn this knowledge to your advantage. Let it help you express your individuality and wholeness.

Do you really want to be a book that gets left on the shelf simply because you felt you were above it all and didn't bother to address your cover? It reminds me of the scene in *The Devil Wears Prada*, where Meryl Streep's formidable character dresses down her new assistant, Andi, played by Anne Hathaway, where she meticulously details the chain of events that led to her assistant making a choice that was determined for her by the fashion world, while simultaneously thinking she was exempt.

None of us who want to really be fully expressed can afford to ignore our external world.

Work with it, not against it, and once again, your life will be easier. And the world will be easier to change. Having choice in this area means you possess a level of technical knowledge to help you manage all the details well. No one figures this stuff out completely on their own—they either have exceptional parents, well-schooled friends or teachers, or professionals to help. Even if they are self-taught, they can still benefit from some expert assistance. Just as with any well-executed building, room, closet, or speech, there are principles of design that need to be in place to achieve a well-rounded physical appearance. Provided you've got the first two elements in the equation (character and congruence) handled, the conscious choice part is easy. Try to approach your presence without it, and you'll find yourself floundering in a sea of fashion without any discernible personality showing. There are many examples of people in our world who have mastered all three Big Cs with big results, whether they were consciously using them or unconsciously going with the flow.

Case in Point

Do you think that Taylor Swift hasn't used every single one of the Three Cs on her journey to becoming an economic and political juggernaut, while holding tightly to her natural adorable qualities that made her relatable right off the hop? Damn right she did, does, and will again! Look, she started out as a kid, singing songs, barely bigger than her guitar and has worked tirelessly to reinvent herself as she grows, without losing her grounding in who she is. Yes, she is a songwriting savant who secured a position at Sony at the tender age of 14, but she is also a highly relatable person. Even when she spent a year in hermitville after getting knocked down, she came out swinging, overtly feminist, and taking back the control of her narrative from those that tried to shift it for their own profit. I mean, she's even loopholing Scooter Braun by re-recording her entire early catalog, thereby dropping the value of the original masters he bought for millions to ZERO. She demonstrates Character in every move she makes.

She's also highly Congruent, putting in the work to support her vision of what she wants for her art. She did a tour on every single album and prepared for it by singing all the sets while running in heels on a treadmill for fast songs and walking for the slow ones. I mean, come on. No one can deny that her mastery of self-knowledge and a willingness to play the contradictions for women in society is one of the most badass moves by a singer-songwriter EVER. She's aware of the pile of expectations on her, and not only skillfully navigates them, she uses them for her art, writing songs like "The Man," where she talks about her qualities such as her assertiveness, dating history, and business savvy, noting that they would be celebrated, not denigrated if she were a man. She writes positive songs, revenge songs, sad songs— there isn't an emotion she hasn't covered and she continually speaks well in interviews, rarely caught off guard.

Yes, she gets a ton of support from her family and their willingness to use their resources to shepherd her talents, but she has seemingly known who she was from a very young age and exercises Choice in all things. She has been able to mold her external world to her internal one and she keeps a tight rein on the details, squarely holding the reins of creative control over her work. As a result, she remains one of the greatest musical stars and savvy businesswomen of our time, and I'm personally curious to see where she'll go next.

The Three Cs work, on any scale you want to play.

Over time, in the form of increased confidence leading to promotions, negotiation wins, smoother relationships, and overall life satisfaction, you'll find yourself far ahead of those who don't bother, or who don't go far enough, and then you're in a good position to change the world.

Your choices matter. Make good ones.

Let's go deeper.

CHAPTER 6

Humanizing How-To's #1–3

The seven Seas

The seven Seas
(Sea of Cs, see?)
of the "get real,"
really,
lead to a place of
whole self
wholly present and,
provided you really dig,
can foundationally found a
whole new life
or way of it that
suits you like bespoke,
spoken word into your soul, which
in a soulless corporate world,
needs a dash of haberdashery,
extra special care,
compartmental now, but
relational soon as you
sail out on these seven,
seas of self-discovery and how,
mapped out, get you from
Point A to BE,
real, really real and
though sailing takes
more time and more
knowledge of the wind and
rain currents roll chop and pitch,

it's so close to
all the other seas and
oceans of selves you'll meet
on the water waves wide so
sail,
sail out on these,
and practice,
the seven,
the seas:
Consciousness
Compassion
Core
Culture
Charm
Connection
Celebration
Each elemental, elementary,
yet,
postdocgraduatelevellearning and
yearning for something more, in
business, a new way of being,
in the journey, the sail we set
for real.

You might have guessed by now that I love to philosophize, visioning a brave new world where we're all just a little more (or a lot more) human and easy on ourselves. What you're going to see now is that I'm also shockingly pragmatic, and I love a good "roll up your sleeves" moment or seven. If you've been spending the last five chapters exasperated because you wanted to cut to the chase, you're in luck. We're getting to it now, with more on the how-to of all this.

Over the next few chapters, we're going to explore the Three Cs in more depth and break them down into seven simple practices to start so you can ease into the work of humanizing yourself. Naturally, the book can't cover everything we work on in programs for this or we'd be giving War and Peace a run for its money on length, but it's better to include the starting point than to just explain the theory and let you figure it out on your own.

For those of you who are seasoned execs, these practices might seem a bit basic, but stick with me—simple is effective.

It's okay to go back to basics. I invite you to slip into your quiet, beginner's mind.

Character: Exploring Your Internal Landscape

#1—Consciousness

Consciousness
the first step on
the boat, boarding
onboarding, awake, watching out
over the prow, proven to change
the range of our goal arrow and
we waken, stretch, alive, enlivened
realize that we are not our bones
body embodied, but spiritual electrics
sparking out over the universe as
we know it and we need it, this
awareness, to even start a shift
as if we knew
all along, we were here
See
Feel
Hear
Taste
Touch
Embodied, bodies and
brainmindheartsoul
we are
aware.

Let's refresh, it's been a while since we talked awareness:

> *The quality or state of being aware especially of something within oneself, the state or fact of being conscious of an external object, state, or fact. A state of being.*
>
> —Merriam Webster

It's one thing to be aware, which is a bit passive, and quite another to be Conscious, which is active.

Now, if you're like me, you're going to breeze through this and not bother actually doing any of the exercises because you'll C them as too simple *(bahahaha)*.

Don't.

Just try it.

I designed it this way on purpose and you'll soon find that I hate fluff as much as you do. Just humor me and do them. You can report back later.

This first practice is designed to take you from simple awareness to active Consciousness, becoming conscious of yourself, your environment, and all the tiny interactions in between.

Keep this in mind:

- I am worthy of clarity for myself and for others.
- Clarity gives access to action.*

Practice #1—Observe and Call Out

In this process, spend a couple of weeks (yes, weeks) simply paying attention to your inner and outer world and making notes on what you see, hear, feel, and think. This process can be called a lot of things, "notice

---

* Thanks to Michael Walsh (Kaizen Consulting) for this little gem! It's helped me many times.

and name," "see and say," "look and label," but it all amounts to the same thing.

It's putting words to what's happening, just the facts.

You can do this just mentally for the first little bit, then say the things you notice out loud and then afterward you may wish to write it down so you can begin to track what's going on. It's particularly good for catching out negative self-talk but can be used with patterns of behavior or communication as well.

Here's how a first simple internal exchange might go:

"Ugh, I look terrible!" (you notice the thought and call it out).

*"Good catch, you!"** (you give yourself props for noticing—this might seem silly, but we want to do things more often and more quickly when we're praised).

That's it, just at the beginning.* Simple, right? Give yourself a week or two and you'll be a pro—your speed will increase, and you'll start to take note more often in the moment of what's happening. Before you can change anything, you need to identify what needs changing, and this is one of the quickest ways to get the information you need.

*Extra Credit: C+

- For extra oomph, try using your name instead of "you." It's a little trick that works because our brains are strangely wired to more readily accept information from the third person voice. "[My name] looks great today!" is always going to be perceived as stronger than "I look great today!"
- For extra–extra oomph, you can write these thoughts down or make a note of how often they're coming up, but it's not strictly necessary. You just keep observing and calling out and appreciating your ability to do so. Why bother? Because dopamine is yummy. Dopamine helps us do hard things and the positive self-talk gives us more dopamine than does negative, so the props will literally prop you up.

Here's two cents:

As you start to become aware of your patterns, habits, feelings, and thoughts, it's entirely possible that you'll be deluged with some negativity. Those internal demons can get pretty loud, especially when you start to make changes. Their job is to keep you safe and maintain the status quo, but they are not to dictate the course of your life from now on. Let them be there, notice them, but don't let them drive—they can sit in the back seat and argue.

#2—Compassion

Compassion,
we recognize
the suffering of others and
ourselves and
act to alleviate because
everything, and
I mean *everything*
changes better
with love.

We all need a little grace from time to time, so to keep this process loving, we need some compassion to get through. Here's the traditional definition:

> *A strong feeling of sympathy and sadness for the suffering or bad luck of others and a wish to help them.*
>
> —Oxford Languages

Now in this case, we will save the sympathy for others until a bit later in the process—right now, I want you to direct all the compassion you have to yourself as you uncover things in your consciousness practice. Be kind.

If you've uncovered something you find you don't like, be gentle. You can always change that thing later, but for now, just notice the thought, pattern, or behavior and let yourself know it's okay to be where you're at.

This second practice is designed to help you establish and mold new brain pathways and boost your "feel-good" potential. Here, you can give yourself some props for learning and remember what the neuroscientists say: positive self-talk while doing something difficult gives you almost twice the dopamine hit than saying nothing or talking negatively.

Keep this in mind:

- I am worthy of gentleness.
- Gentleness gives me fuel for my growth.

Once we've gotten good at calling out the negative thought patterns, we can offer ourselves some compassion and work to reframe those negative thoughts in a more positive light. Here's where you take what you've noticed and make the change in your thinking. It's really about giving your brain something else to do besides keep thinking the same old things.

This is what a sample internal dialogue might sound like:

> *"Ugh, I look terrible!"* (notice the thought and call it out).
> *"Good catch, you!"* (give yourself props for noticing).

"Hey, that isn't a thought I want to keep thinking!" (start the change process).

"What can I think instead, that would be more helpful?" (choose a different path).

"I noticed that my shirt's color really complimented my personal coloring and it fit me really well!" (give your brain another thought to think instead).

Wash, rinse, repeat.

Wash, rinse, repeat.

You've heard the proverb about "Before enlightenment, chop wood, carry water. After enlightenment, chop wood, carry water." It's like that. There are actions that you just need to keep doing, moment by moment, day by day, until they are second nature in order to make a shift.

You'll find that after a while you'll be observing changed thinking, just from working through this simple process on repeat. You can use this process for behaviors and actions as well to help gently shift the neural pathways to new ones.

Here's an extra two cents:

Keep in mind that this will feel tough. Your regular, well-worn neural pathways will feel like an eight-lane freeway with easy on-and-off ramps and express lanes. The new ones will feel like hacking through a jungle with a machete to make a new path.

Keep going and soon the new paths of thinking will be more easily and consistently traversable.

Once your new pathways are in good condition, it's time to start looking for the other parts of your character—investigating your strengths and skills, your values, and your vision. Equipped with a positive outlook, you can go digging with a more balanced view of the things you are great at and the things you need to work on. All of getting real starts with character, for good or ill.

#3—Core

Core
where we
never change
where we sit,
ensouled
enshrined at the middle
of who we are now and then
and before now and then and
who we were before we got here
and who we'll be when we leave
who you are at four is who you are
at one hundred and four and with
awareness and love, you can dig dig dig
down deep to the heart and melt into the molten
depths and find the child and the adult and the wild
in the dark, in the light, of the core.

Finally, the last piece of this chunk of work is to go to the Core—you want to really dig in to see what you brought with you, what you learned, and who you are at the heart of yourself. It's a bit of an excavation of the past and an acceptance of all the gifts and skills you brought with you into the world. This is your chance to really pinpoint what makes you unique and is the foundation for all the other work of getting real. Let's do another definition, just for fun, of "core":

The part of something that is central to its existence or character.
—Oxford Languages

Your core is who you were at four and who you will be at a hundred and four.

Looking at the gifts you came into the world with will give you an idea of the gifts you can use now to be fully expressed as your whole self. When you understand your past and present, you can better shape your future.

You cannot humanize yourself and your work without first fully understanding your strengths, weaknesses, foibles, quirks, and unique gifts.

Parts of your core are either inherent or inherited. Both nature and nurture play a part here and all parts of yourself can, thankfully, be developed. I believe in the power of starting with your strengths, acknowledging your weaknesses, and making plans to maximize one and minimize the other.

This third practice is designed for you to get as much information as you can about who you are internally so you can decide how you want to express yourself accurately. There are any number of ways to investigate your core, including a variety of personality tests, external feedback, and other measures, but for now, just work on a short list of your attributes to start. It's far easier to build on strengths than fix weaknesses, so let's go for the easy win—this will make it much easier to withstand the storms of external opinion and help bolster your self-esteem for the times when you get a bit overwhelmed with the expectations of the world you inhabit.

Case in Point

I was always headstrong; I was born that way. Sometimes that's great and sometimes it gets me into trouble when I'd rather be right and am absolutely sure that my way is the only way. When I have those days, I use compassion to remind myself that I'm learning to use that headstrong nature when I need it and tame it when I need flexibility instead. —KL (Okay, this is a case from my personal experience, but it's true!)

Keep this in mind:

- Understanding my core will help accelerate my growth and development.
- Who I am is central to the way I will be in the world.

Practice: Who am I when nobody is looking?

To start looking at your Core, there are some key questions I use with clients regularly that you can use as well to get started. Get out a journal or piece of paper or your tablet or phone notes and write down these questions:

1. Who am I when nobody is looking?
2. What do I really do well?
3. What do I really love to do?
4. What do I really want when nobody is looking?
5. What gifts did I get for free?

You might be wondering why I include the phrase "when nobody is looking." I add it because so many of the people I work with are heavily influenced by the others around them, family, friends, kids, and so on. Few of them genuinely get to spend any time alone with themselves and their thoughts. For you to get right back to where you started and truly understand yourself, you have to think about what you would do if you were only responsible to and for yourself and no one else. This exercise is often quite joyful for people, as they all generally carry a fair amount of responsibility and have a strong sense of duty. If you cannot describe who you are, what you like, and what you want when nobody's looking, then you probably don't know your core all that well. On top of that, it's hard to advocate for yourself and develop your gifts when you are starting from a place of the unknown. I'm not suggesting you abandon others at all, but for this exercise, it's best to consider only yourself.

You can also access a wide variety of external assessments to help you find your way—I personally like a mix of the somewhat scientific and what many people affectionately (or not so affectionately) call "woo-woo," because who doesn't like to have a little fun?

Try some of these on for size:

- True Colors (this one is a bit woo, but interesting).
- Astrology (it can be fun), either Western or Chinese or Indian or other.
- Myers–Briggs (largely debunked as a form of evaluation for hiring but can be interesting for a starting place for personality archetype).
- DISC (I find this one very linear, good for concrete thinkers).
- Strengths Deployment Inventory (I like this one because it shows not only your general leadership tendencies but also what you'll do in conflict).
- Insights (this one is pretty comprehensive, but can feel a bit generic in its comments so it's best debriefed by the analyst).
- Enneagram (there are a ton of books on this one).
- Gene Keys (this is more about your soul's path and getting to the heart of your work in the world and it gives you things to contemplate for the journey).
- Akashic Records (this is fun if you like the idea of spirit guides—apparently mine are like bees in a lilac bush, busy, fragrant, and constantly laughing at/with me, delighted).
- Three-hundred-and sixty-degree assessments for direct external feedback (I don't love these in the automated format, as they're

kind of impersonal and sometimes serve as a venting space, but curated questions of key relationships in your world can be useful for seeing any blind spots).

- Clifton Strengthsfinders (this one is great for giving you a succinct, five-word list of your main strengths and good explanations on how to use them).
- Human Design (gives you an idea of how your energy system works and is connected to your physical being).
- Cosmo and BuzzFeed quizzes (I'm kidding, these can be fun but maybe not to be taken too seriously).

The list is endless, as there are always new things popping up in our world as ways for us to know ourselves. See which ones resonate with you.

Here's an extra two cents:

Once you've tried a few of these things, be cautious about their application to your life. I often hear people saying something like, "I am a _____" instead of "I lead with _____" or "My personality tends to operate with this kind of energy." No personality test can define you fully and nothing is set in stone. The purpose of all of these things is simply to give you different perspectives, different mirrors, and different angles to help you explore and define for yourself who you are and how you roll in the world.

If you don't know yourself

If you don't know yourself
you can't know the world,
can't see it in all the dimensions
and diversions and just won't have
the capacity to understand,
like those tribes who didn't know
what a boat was when they saw it
and sure didn't know it was their
doom and if you don't know yourself
you'll be doomed to wander, pinball
bashing from paddle to post
knocked by the flippers of fate into
rails you didn't see coming and always
reacting, not acting so know this,
when you're known, you know.

CHAPTER 7

Humanizing How-To's #4–5

Congruence

Congruence
is the balancing of the
internalexternal world
of who you are with
what they expect and
you need a bit of both,
to help people make sense
of the sense that's you.

Congruence: Exploring Your External Influences

Remember that old joke by David Foster Wallace with the two small fishes swimming by the big fish when the big fish asks them, "How's the water?" and they respond, "Water?" If you are unaware of your environment, you'll miss the effects of its influence on you as well as the expectations of the people in it and that's half the equation of getting real. Before we get to the practices that will help you with this, keep these next few things in mind.

The lenses through which we see ourselves matter.

Which mirror are you using

Which mirror are you using
my dear darling soul, when
formulating the form of your
beingdoinghaving?
Is it the form of the world obsessed with
appearances, wealth, and worldliness, or
the form of your family, and all they thought, or
that of your friends moving into passion projects and
trying to get by without getting down?
You areandalwayswillbe reflected in the eyes of others but
know that their view is sometimes skewed and you need to
choose your mirrors carefully.
Ideally, your parents installed accurate mirrors, internal voices
clear and kind, but for those of us with funhouse mirrors,
odd distortions, and strange, we need to take
special care, to choose our friend mirrors for help
when we help
ourselves to clearer
reflections.

External feedback is a useful tool; don't let it become a prison.

It's a bit dangerous to just go to the court of public opinion for external feedback/validation. You'll likely get hung out to dry or ripped apart by the dogs of keyboard warriors who have nothing better to do than sow misery. Pay close attention to **who** you're using as a mirror. Sometimes your family is great, and sometimes they stink. Sometimes coaches look like experts for others, but they won't work for you. Choose good mirrors.

One more thing...

Our past can and does

Our past can and does
affect us
until
we can
spot all the tender spots
of patterns repeating and
reactions coming hard and fast
to something that's soft and slow
and we all know if it's
hysterical
it's
historical and so,
any look to the present or future
complete, must necessarily
take a look at the past,
unless of course,
you're one of those shiny golden souls
who had a perfect childhood and got out
with all yourself intact.

I know many people who would prefer to cling to the belief that "the past is past," but that's not how our hearts and minds work.

Anyone who says their past doesn't impact their current life is lying somewhere, to themselves or to you.

Experiences from the past shape our beliefs, attitudes, perceptions, and actions. Whether they came from our childhood upbringing, our education, our relationships or various successes, failures and trauma, these experiences create patterns of thinking and behaving that have a marked effect on the choices we make and the outcomes we receive in the present moment. If we've experienced a lot of negativity, we can approach new experiences with increased self-doubt. If, on the flipside, we experience positive things, we will feel more confident to take a new course of action.

While it's impossible to rewrite history, it is crucial we recognize and transform the impact that these past patterns have on our lives.

If we can acknowledge and reframe our negative experiences, we can shift our emotions, perspectives, and beliefs to get a better understanding of ourselves and develop different ways of thinking that are more likely to get us where we want to go. It can be both empowering and frightening to think about and reach this level of growth, but it is essential for fostering a deep connection to ourselves and others. Naturally, we don't do this kind of internal excavation alone, and a variety of approaches may be helpful— therapy of various kinds, reading personal development books (like this one), talking things out with friends and family, getting assistance from coaches or spiritual advisers and using their input to contemplate where we came from. We also can use these connections to understand our culture more fully and examine how it shaped us and continues to shape us. We really need to get a grip on where we're situated so we can make some conscious choices on where to go and what to do next.

#4—Culture

Culture,
where we live, not
in a vacuum, alone, but
together,
we must consider
who we are within
the system of bins of
compartments
contextual and
consensual and
raceclasssmarts
sense geographical
familialfamiliar and
foreign and
where did we come from
as a group
as a member
a finger on a hand
of a body
where we live
on the earth
in community, communing,
musicfoodcostumedifference
and believe what they believed
and see how it shaped
youmeandallofmeusthemthen
and how it holdsheldmoved us,
molded into shapes of
subjects that made us
us.

This fourth practice is designed for you to get an accurate and as complete as possible picture of your current landscape by exploring your world. This will help you with your choices later about how you want to align your internal world with the external world's expectations.

Keep this in mind:

- We don't live in a vacuum.
- The things outside of me have shaped me.

Practice: What Is Your Culture?

Start with a journaling or listing exercise to begin to understand your cultural influences. What outside of you has influenced you and continues to influence you today? Here are a few prompts to help:

1. Where do I live (home, neighborhood, city, state/province/territory, country, continent)?
2. What is my cultural background (ethnicity, spirituality, race)?
3. What do I really value?
4. How are my values the same or different from my family?
5. What is my family system (parents, siblings, extended family)?
6. What is my community system (friends, hobbies, spiritual groups, other social)?
7. What is my work (company, industry, location, hours, style)?
8. What expectations are placed on me based on all these factors?

Once you've done the lists, then you can begin to look for the lines between your internal desires and your external desires for expression. The purpose here is for you to begin to consider how and what you want to express as you bring your internal world into alignment with your external world. If you like visuals, you can try creating a Venn Diagram (Figure 7.1)—take all your abovementioned lists and compare them with what you believe, think, and feel internally.

Spend some time with your diagram and see where "who you are" and "what you like" overlaps with the expectations of your industry, your

My work in the world as a banker:

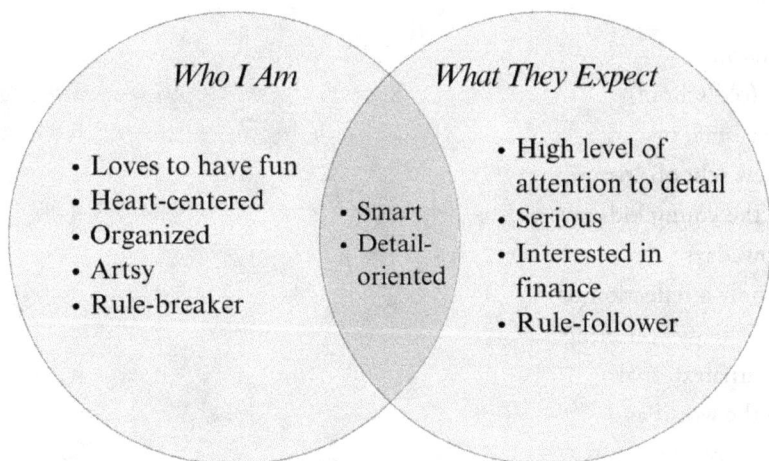

Not a lot of overlap, probably need a different job.

Figure 7.1 Venn Diagram showing different characteristics and their overlap as an example

profession, your city, your country, and your social location. If they don't overlap much, you probably need a new career. If they're highly linked, you're good to go. If they're somewhere in the middle, you'll have to figure out how to exist in a context that still works with your unique self.

Here's an extra two cents:

In certain contexts, it won't be safe for you to step outside the box as much as you'd like. In these cases, do whatever you need to do to keep yourself alive, whole and sane. If you have the opportunity to get to another place where you're safer, please do so. I also recognize that this kind of work is only possible when you have the privilege and safety to do it, so if you're in a tough spot, please be kind to yourself and go as slowly as you need to go.

#5—Charm

Charm
or (old school)
charisma, or
(new school) 'rizz,
as the young kids say
nowadays
is only a reflection of
the energy you bring
internalexternal
to the world and
how your fizzy bits
come into a room and
change the dynamic for
good or ill.
How you interact
with yourselfothers is how
you interact with the world
so
it's so important to
make sure your
being, in all ways
appearing,
behaving,
speaking,
is turned on,
plugged in, and
transmitting.
Signals.

Charm is such a lovely way to think of your "being" in the world. The definition of it is "the power or quality of giving delight or *arousing admiration*," or when used as a verb, "to delight greatly." I think the idea of you coming into this world to delight it greatly is fantastic. I want to be delighted by you! I am delighted by you! I want the world to know you better. Cultivating your charm is one of the quickest ways to tell the world who you are without saying a word.

People like it when people make sense

This fifth practice is where the tangible aspects of image begin to play a role. You can express your Charm by using your clothing, your personal body care and maintenance, your voice, your body language, your personality style, the way you speak, and the words you use. It can also inform other peripheral things such as your style of home, your mode of transportation, your hobbies and activities, and even the people you hang out with and where you live. It's really about expressing all the things that are unique to you and having fun while you're doing it. This is a place to begin making friends with your internal and external landscapes and to create harmony between them as you get congruent between what you want and what the world expects of you.

Your charm can be delicate, prickly, quirky, soft or edgy, or anything else you can think of, but no matter what, your charm is always going to be uniquely you.

Charm Is Attractive

Let's be clear. Being attractive is an advantage to you, so developing your Charm is helpful in terms of expressing who you are and helping people understand you.

It's a powerful tool

It's a powerful tool,
being attractive, and
not dependent specifically on
the way you look,
physically speaking
(thankfully)
since many of us are
solidly in the average
when it comes to looks
(which is funny because
models generally
have mathematically
average faces,
proportionally speaking).
Though not all of
us can be godlike,
physically perfect,
we can all harness the
power of our own
attractiveness
(whatever that is)
your own
specialsauce
combinationmeal
with fries, a drink, and all the
delicious things.
Yum.

Attractive is a wide umbrella.

It's not just about looks, and thank goodness, otherwise those of us that are a solid 6 on the scale of 1 to 10 on the physical beauty scale would be in trouble. Don't get me wrong, the physical definitely helps, and dressing, caring for, and adorning yourself according to your body type, coloring, and personality is a game changer in the world of attraction, but your attitude, actions, and outlook all play a part too.

Developing your charm is good for you.

People who are perceived as more attractive are often seen as more competent, offered more opportunities to grow, and earn more money. It's linked to greater relationship satisfaction, higher self-esteem, and more life satisfaction in general.

Don't just take my word for it though...

- Attractive workers are considered more able—Mobius and Rosenblat.[27]
- Attractive workers earn 10 to 15 percent more—Hamermesh and Biddle.[28]
- Your promotability is 15 percent skill set, 85 percent presence—Riborg–Mann.[29]

(The studies have been around for more than a hundred years, and the last one I just mentioned is from 1918! You'd think we'd have gotten it by now.)

The bottom line is:

Nature doesn't make mistakes. Whatever container you're in is the perfect container to do whatever you're meant to do on the planet.

The sooner you make friends with your container and become comfortable in your own skin, the easier your life is going to roll.

Keep this in mind:

- Everything I do contributes to my overall being in the world.
- My being deserves accurate and fulfilling expression.

Exploration: Delight Greatly

Writing/thinking prompts:

1. Considering everything you've learned about yourself and your world up to this point, how well does your inside world align with your outside world?
2. What do you want the world to know about you or to "get" about you? This could be strengths, skills, talents, or something else about your personality.
3. What are the vehicles you want to use to express yourself as a whole, humanized person?

Here's another two cents:

As you make your charming choices, consider yourself, your role, your company, your industry, and your life outside work. If you're a parent, you'll have additional dimensions to consider, since most of your choices will need to be highly durable/childproof and versatile for switching between the boardroom and the soccer field. If you're a child-free individual who drives from parking garage to parking garage to work in a high-level office and never sees sticky fingers, you can afford the vicuna sports coat. (Seriously though, with the price of vicuna at almost $4,000 per yard and its delicacy, just buy a fine, highly durable wool coat and save yourself the heartache of pilling and wear.)

May I speak plainly?

- *We need to rely on both our inner compass and outer validation.*
- *To calibrate your compasses, you need to understand yourself and your values clearly.*
- *Sometimes, starting from the outside in is not a bad path to follow.*

Dolly Parton is the GOAT*

Dolly Parton is the GOAT,
sitting atop a mountain of
picking guitar strings and
singular voice, nails and hair
hips and sharp thinking,
underestimated and
views understated but
lived large in donations of
books and tuition and all the
kindest things, lifting up,
doing good while doing well and
always sticking to the point,
playing her lane, unparalleled,
entertainment entrained, but
sure as poor origin story to
Grand Ole Opry, never misstepping,
well governed and never fazed, never
touching topics, talking after school, gossip and
graciously deflecting and inside,
steel knowing, I AM, supported, and
never wavering, knows exactly
who
she
is,
and lives accordingly.

---

* Greatest Of All Time—and yes, she is one of the best examples of congruence in the world today.

CHAPTER 8

Humanizing How-To's #6–7

Choice: Exploring Your Expression in the World

Everything is a Choice

Everything is a Choice,
you get to decide,
how you act,
how you think,
how you speakwalktalk
be
your real self, embodied,
a choice, deliberate, and
all the little things add up
over time, and though we know
there are expectations,
your expectation of what to meet
and when, is the only real choice
that counts.

All of the things you decide about how you want to express yourself are important. No detail is too small. All those small details add up to the impression and impact you make in the world and a significant part of getting real.

How you connect with the world affects the quality of your life.

#6—Connection

Connection
is the only way
any of us are
going to meet in the middle
of this polarized world and
this process of connecting
yourself with your world,
testing your real self-expression out on
the people you meet
and seeing yourself
reflected, is a
blessing, freeing, and
now is not the time to
hide but
to shine, so
act to connect and
watch for the
real results.

This sixth practice is about getting some rubber on the road, testing out the vehicles you wanted to use for your self-expression in #5 and how they interact with the world to create a good connection with others. These practices are meant to be a starting point of investigation, not an exhaustive list. Believe me, I could write an entire book on just this alone, but it would give War and Peace a run for its money, and I don't want to scare you.

Take your time, go slowly, and get help if needed.

Keep this in mind:

- I deserve to be seen, heard, and valued.
- My real self is a useful vehicle for communicating who I am to others.
- When I clearly communicate as my real congruent self, I can connect better with my world.

Whenever you meet with someone, whether a friend, colleague, family, or stranger, a relationship is formed. Connection is the point where we decide how much of ourselves to share and how real we want to be. The fact is when I show up as my real self, congruent, and you do too, then we have a chance at a true relationship where we're both seen, heard, and valued.

> **The choices we make with our appearance, behavior, and communication affect the quality of our connections.**

People like to understand one another, and they like it when they can do it quickly. If your appearance is accurate, meaning that it clearly reflects your true self, your inner world, then this helps to speed up the connection with others. At first glance, people will be unconsciously deciding whether you are alike, not alike, safe, not safe, and whether they want to pursue a further connection with you simply based on the way you look. I've tested this with hundreds of audiences and can definitively say that everyone has a "best guess" about you, based on their own information.

Case in Point

When I talk to audiences about the importance of the visual, I ask them to evaluate four people's pictures on a slide, people who have different genders, different races, and different styles of clothing. The results are always the same—the blonde with the short skirt is always in "entertainment" of some kind, the tall good-looking man in a suit is always a player who is dating many women, the young man in a tee shirt and crossbody bag is always a student and the woman with crossed arms in a suit is always in a professional services role and is always seen as unlikeable by her colleagues. This is just a small sample of the answers people give and the answers might vary a little, but the patterns are always the same. People have ideas in their heads like giant filing cabinets, based on the information they've gathered over the years from all the different sources, their family, their culture, and so on.

At the same time…

Appearance is just a vehicle

Appearance is just a vehicle,
a tiny amuse bouche
appetizer, taste tasty, to
whet the appetites of
the people you meet,
to make you make sense to
them and then
when you do,
they know, like, and trust you
faster and that,
that is a speed worth having.

People tend to consider appearance superficial, which misses the point completely.

Image is surface, but it is not superficial.

We know that our being encompasses more than our meat suit, but our meat suit is part of our human experience. Since we're focusing on humanizing and fully expressing ourselves with these practices, we need to pay our outsides some kind and loving attention. When you show up unabashedly and exactly as you are, you have way more energy to BE with the people in the rooms, instead of spending your energy on maintaining your walls. The beauty of it is that your appearance can be aligned with our deeper being to express your real self effectively before you even say a word.

Underneath it all

Underneath it all
values are
what counts and
your outsides should
reflect your insides,
accurately.
All the things of you, the
way you move in
the world, and
all the little quirks,
quarky, and
power, yes power,
fairy dust or
stone, and
the way you think and feel,
can all be summed up in
a visual expression but
at the heart of it,
wear your values on
your sleeve
on your skirtshirthat and
pants it up!
Be free.

Underneath it all, values are what count: your outsides should reflect your insides accurately. If you're a serious person, your appearance can indicate that in darker colors and more conservative clothing. If you're highly creative, you can show it in eclectic combinations of pattern, texture, and style. Whatever you choose, it has to reflect you.

At the same time, be aware:

Image only matters where it matters.

When you're at home with your family, or on the beach enjoying a sunny day, or hanging out with your friends, focusing on your image is less important than being present with the ones you love, taking in the beauty of the moment. If you're on camera or in person for work or some important occasion, then that's a different story. You are in a place where you are specifically seeking to make a particular impression.

Image only matters where it matters, but *when* it matters, we need to give it the level of respect and attention it deserves as a highly effective tool for communication and connection.

#6a: Appearance

1. Wardrobe assessment—Use your camera and a mirror to capture your daily outfits for at least two weeks. Make a note each day of how you felt about what you were wearing, both emotionally and physically, how people reacted to you and what, if any, comments and reactions you received. Once your data gathering is finished, start looking back through it to identify patterns and see what insights you can gain. Are you always wearing the same thing? Did things change if you tried something different, perhaps a different outfit or a different level of formality (more casual or more formal)? Do you feel happy with your clothing choices? Did you feel connected to yourself as a leader? Explore all of these questions and decide if there's room for change.

2. Body assessment—In this exercise, you're working with the principles of design in your body, things such as color, shape, line, texture, weight (of fabrics and accessories, not of you), and sheen. The key

thing to remember here is your body is the perfect indicator to tell you what will look good on your body. **Match your body to what you're putting on it.** If you're short, you're going to look best in short things. If your body is soft, then soft fabrics will suit you best. If your coloring is bright and vibrant, then bright colors will work best on you. If your body has straight lines, then the lines of your clothing will be straight (like sharply tailored suits). Spend a bit of time looking in the mirror to discern your personal design elements and check your closet to see if the clothing in it matches you. When everything you wear matches your body, it's easier and less vulnerable to be seen by others. Pay attention to how you feel and how you're being received by others when you wear what matches you.

3. Personality style—Using the assessments from earlier in the book, check your wardrobe to see if it matches you. For example, if you're quite a serious person, then your wardrobe is likely going to feel best if your clothing is very simple, a bit more formal, and a bit darker with fewer colors. If you're quite a creative person, then your wardrobe is likely going to feel best when it's full of color and eclectic pieces. How well does your wardrobe align with you and your world? How are you perceived when you wear things that match your personality? Does it need a bit of shifting? Is your clothing matching the full expression of your personality?

Play around with all of these aspects of your physical image and see what happens. Keep what you like and leave the rest.

Here's an extra two cents…

Whenever I get into the image piece with my leaders, I always find myself getting into the psychology surrounding the choices we make when it comes to clothing. Old patterns of insecurity, body dysmorphia, worthiness, and status jump up from that pile of clothes that don't fit, or the dusty, outdated pieces in the back of the closet. Just be mindful of the fact that your closet can surprise you. Remember, as we talk connection…

There's always more

There's always more
in the closet
than clothes,
more than just the
outward expression of
our inward selves, it's a
mix of psychology, physiology
faith and fear,
indications of our
worthiness, fits of
insecurity and body image
issues, displays of status
and all kinds of societal
pressures that ask us to be more
or less or more or less what we are
or are not and the expectation of the
closet to fulfill a simple containment
purpose is mistaken, a myth of
mythic proportions when our
proportions aren't proportional or
our thoughts aren't containable and
there is always
always
more in the closet
than clothes.

Like anything, a focus on image can be taken too far—you need enough of a focus to ensure that your image is well aligned with who you are, but not so much that you're constantly having to change what you wear and how you show up based on trends, societal expectations, and a desire to please others. We all have societal requirements on us to show up in a particular way, but too much reliance on the social norms can inhibit your expression and therefore your connection with others.

A lack of self-acceptance can result if your particular characteristics don't fall into the societal norms of what is considered attractive, and this can lead to lowered self-esteem. Once you're there, you end up in a vicious cycle of trying to fit in and make people like you, and you lose your identity in the process.

Did you see Madonna's new face*

Did you see Madonna's new face,
stretched thin
skinned across angular bones
artificially inflated filler
shocked and full-lipped
destruction of the original,
desecration and
delusional youth,
irrelevant and
trying way too hard and sure
she's a great example of
why that strict focus on image is
so dangerous…
it's passing,
passing for something, and
so many women and
a few men, not many,
are sucked into
the maw of manipulation, of
excessive messing, with the
face Nature gave them and
Botoxic bumps masquerading as
cheeks and forehead,
wrinkleless weirdness and
so far out of the norm,
whatever that is,
seems like a cry for congruence
from someone who
maybe never really had it and
when you place
all your base of
operations on your face,
you'll eventually fall.

No amount of plastic suspension
can keep you
from sixtyseventy,
onehundredandtwo and
finally,
chasing death.
Weirdly, we don't mind "work," as
long as we don't see it
obvious,
but
are sad
when we see something
beautifulartistry,
mauled into masks,
claylike and false,
because we told them
they weren't
worthy
without
it.

---

* Poke: Yeah, I know, this poem is a little judgy of me. I'm sad that women still have to smooth, lift, tighten or do anything else with their bodies and faces to be seen as attractive. I'd love more representation of what it looks like to be 50 and over without the benefit of celebrity trainers, nutritionists, stylists, etc. I mean, work what you have, for sure, but don't kill yourself trying.

Your image is a part of the journey but never the destination.

Pay attention, but don't drive off the road.

Now let's talk about the way you behave…

Your actions create or destroy

Your actions create or destroy
connection, your attitude,
your life, and
all the little things.
Living in the material world, we
act and act and act and
big or small, it's the
only thing that
moves us forward
and so,
be cognizant, cogent of
your actions because
they reflect your thoughts and
your values and
tell the people around you,
our society,
what you believe and
you can take them
lightly and walk heavily, but
whatever you do,
consider
the choice:
create or destroy?

Once you're congruent in terms of your appearance, your actions are the thing that drives your engagement with the world at large and you can choose whether to build or destroy connection with every interaction. Like your appearance, your actions need to align with your values, and you need to be consistent in your behavior in order to truly connect with people.

Building connection takes time and focus.

It's not about grand gestures; it's about the small, daily deposits in the action bank. Be kind to yourself and others, extend grace, and make sure your actions match your real self. Do what you say you're going to do when you say you're going to do it. If you promise your colleague you'll have a report ready by Friday, deliver it by Friday, and you've just earned some connection points.

Your actions need to align with your values and you need to act consistently to build connection.

Lady Gaga and the Dalai Lama

Lady Gaga and the Dalai Lama
sat down to talk one day and
the way they both
walked down the
conversational path to
lead to the
conclusion that
kindness was the
only way we'd all get
out of this mess
was such a tidy dance
down the conversational cobblestones,
bordered with segues and
full of dust between and,
talking about taking action,
you can see her living it always,
in her softness to singing with
Tony Bennett, bending to
Liza Minelli with a quiet
"I got you" on a great loud stage,
kind, in kind.
You might not think a
pop star and a
religious leader have a
lot in common but
when kindness is the thread,
we can all relax into
the weavewoven
rug of human fug and
simply helphaul,
hold one another and
intimacy over indifference and
mercy over might and

all the other
dirty deeds done
dirt cheap, falling
falling, away.
Lady Gaga's walking the path,
little monsters, and
wouldn't you rather
we all
stepped as lightly
with love?

#6b: Behavior

1. Try a few behavioral experiments over a two-week period—try being extraordinarily kind or a bit short with people (carefully here, you can play a bit without causing harm) and see the difference. Try showing up extra early to things or just a few minutes late (in low stakes situations, naturally). Try sticking to your promises to yourself concerning exercise or self-care and then try breaking them.

2. At the end of the experiment, note how you felt in each situation. How well did your behavioral choices contribute to your results? What, if anything, needs shifting to bring it into better alignment with the person you are or say you want to be?

#6c: *Communication*

Words and more than words

Words and more than words
on the page, on the stage on the
TV screen movie newspaper writtenscribed
are sticky, so sticky, and sticksandstones
breaking bones might be a fact but
words can break too so we must be
responsible with our choices and
in person and at work, a careless string
of any kind of words spread out anywhere
can hurt others, hurt you, hurt your chances
of advancement or placement or any teamwork
you might want to have, so
choose your words carefully because
they create worlds.

No matter what conversations you're in, with yourself or with others, your words have an impact. First, they help us have precision over pandemonium. If you've ever played the Telephone game where a whispered phrase ends up as a jumbled mess, barely related to the original message, you've experienced firsthand the effect of using the correct words versus approximations. If we're not careful with our words we end up in a mess. Try being very precise with your words and a little less precise and see what happens.

Second, words are the brush you use to paint your intentions—choosing them with empathy can turn a wrecking ball into a feather. Imagine, instead of saying "You're wrong" in a disagreement, you say "I see where you're coming from and here's my perspective." One is bound to ruffle the feathers of your conversational partner and the other is likely to open the door to further discussion. Try a few different conversational gambits and see the results.

Words also have this sneaky way of turning into verbal landmines, waiting to explode when triggered. Carefully chosen words can navigate you through the minefield of sensitive topics, fostering harmony instead of havoc. Your words have the power to uplift or deflate, inspire or crush spirits. Choosing more positive words can be a catalyst for motivation and change. Give it a try with different word choices, either spoken or written, and see what happens.

Exploration: Observe First, Speak After, Repeat

1. Spend two weeks noting your interactions with others in your world. How did your tone of voice, written communication, and body language help or hinder the success of your meetings? Try speaking at different paces, pitches, and volumes. Try open, relaxed body language (keep breathing) or closed. Try shorter, succinct writing and speaking and then try expanding your thoughts. Observe the reactions of those around you and decide what is going to work for you or not. At the same time, check out your social media and online presence—is it communicating in line with who you say you are?

Words help clarify your intentions and they can also shape your reality.

The more you repeat a particular narrative, the more it becomes your truth. Choosing words that affirm and motivate can set the stage for personal success.

P!nk is great for kids

P!nk is great for kids,
because, in singing
her own songs,
colorful,
she's defining the
anti thing,
antithetical,
and calls it out,
outright,
she's not Britney but
still successful
in her own way and
the way she talks
to her own kids, video close,
is reflectively good,
showing how to gently go
in a world determined to be awful and
she sings of body positive, self-positive, and
anthems of joy and support to all those
without
and we all need cheerleaders sometimes.

Your looks and words need to follow your deeds to create a congruent image, build and create trust, and inspire change.

#7—*Celebration*

Celebration
we must
spend a little time,
a lot
looking at how far we've come
applauding the courage, the
action of the self that decided to
cure what ailed it and do the
sometimes painful
work of
getting real, no facade,
all flawed yet pure and
yay! jumpjoy for fullness and
fire and candles lit on celebration's
cake, aside from the satisfaction of
being at a point, inflected, of rest
reflected, we must
(we must)
celebrate!

This practice is designed to keep you motivated to continue honing your alignment, to keep moving forward, and to attract more of what you want into your life. It may feel a bit weird at first to be actively celebrating even just the smallest things, but believe me, you'll get comfortable with it quickly when you see the results. We often spend so much time looking up the mountain at where we think we need to go, that we forget to stop and look down at where we've come from. What we miss is that looking up all the time is exhausting and it's pretty tiring to always be thinking of the next thing on the list. It's energizing to look at the things you've already done.

Keep this in mind:

- I have come a long way in my personal and professional growth.
- I will be more motivated to continue growing as I encourage myself by celebrating my wins, both large and small.
- I am worthy of validation and encouragement.

Exploration: Make Time and Make Lists

1. Book some time in your calendar to reflect on all the things you did over the past week, month, or year. Choose a timeframe that works for you to start. You can even look at the things you did just from the start of working with this book until now.
2. During that time, list out all your accomplishments—these can be small wins or large, big things or little. I remember a time in my life when things were tough and just taking a shower and feeding myself were huge accomplishments. It's okay to celebrate just getting the bare minimum done, and it's okay to celebrate the big things too. You can even celebrate making the time to celebrate!
3. For each thing, stop and write or say or do something celebratory that works for you. Some of my clients like to dance it out or write "Yay you!" beside each thing or say things such as "I'm proud of myself for _____" to themselves. Do it for each accomplishment and thank yourself for sticking to the work.

Speaking of celebration, congratulations, you've reached the end of the Seven Humanizing Seas!

Good leaders are as self-aware and well-regulated as possible to be ready to handle anything life and work throws at them, and getting real (humanizing) is the quickest way to both.

Now, after all this, I can hear you thinking…

Great, Lazaruk, I'm aligned, expressive, and showing up to the table with my whole self. What do I do with my team at work when they all show up as their whole selves too?

Don't worry, we're in the home stretch now. Let's talk about how this works at work.

CHAPTER 9

Humanizing Works at Work

So great, you're all done.* You're humanized. You're a living example of executive being, not just executive presence, and now you've got to show up at work.

What do you do now that you're still working in a world that isn't humanized, yet?

(After all, **they** haven't read the book).

How do you encourage executive being in others?

(I'll give you a hint).

You have the power to change how you do business. Use it.

We will work better together when we understand and accept the people around us in their totality and they understand and accept us in ours.

It starts with you.

---

* Poke: Honestly, I find it hilarious when anyone claims to be fully self-actualized and that they've done all their work. We all have more to learn.

Having this knowledge

Having this knowledge
whole person, present,
helps when we don't agree,
can't see the way
out of our tangles and
knots, set
sailing against the
winds of each other's
blustery hurricanes, how?
Well,
when I know me and
you know you and
you know me and
I know you,
deeply,
then we can see
furtherfaster and
remove ego and
fear and sit with,
not against,
each other
while we wrangle out
the truth of the situation(s) and
sometimes
the best questions are
curious,
no judgment, and
learning, learning,
learn.

To what are you committed?

To what are you committed?
Values, people, words, mission statements
purpose, passion and profit, product driving
production, off the cliff of greedy shores, or
people and their foibles, humanity and
slowing down some, narrowing gaps to
benefit more than one percent and really
digging into what matters now?
To what are you committed?
How would we know?

Remember way back when I said there's a lot going wrong in business and the world? Remember the Big O and how it's shifting on us from hierarchical, authoritarian, and compartmentalized to integrated, relational, and whole? Remember how I said society isn't a thing outside of us, but within us?

Humanizing in the face of inhumanity is courageous as hell.

Wanna go a little further?

(This is not the end. I'm gonna Lord of the Rings you a little here.)
If you're up for it, you might want to play a bigger game…

May I speak plainly?

Humanized workplaces don't:

- *Treat their values like a buffet where they can pick and choose what suits the occasion; they pick a few dishes and eat them.*
- *Claim to value innovation but stifle every idea that comes along; they encourage creativity and mistakes.*
- *Say excellence is their thing then settle for mediocrity; they keep moving toward the target.*

Humanized leaders don't:

- *Bark orders from an ivory tower; they roll up their sleeves and get to work with their people.*
- *Act like machines; they make it okay to be human. Messy, unpredictable, gloriously human.*
- *Waver in their commitment to being human and whole; they go forward boldly, being willing to continue the work daily.*

Being committed means you will hold everyone accountable to change, from the top brass to the interns, but gently.

If someone's not pulling their weight or is straying from the values, call them out. Ensure that everyone is responsible for the success and integrity of the organization and of the people in it.

It's just good business.

But don't take my word for it:

- According to Deloitte's Purpose Premium paper, 65 percent of Americans believe that, in addition to the board of directors and stockholders, CEOs should also hold themselves accountable to the public.[30]
- Glassdoor reports that 77 percent of job seekers prioritize company culture over salary. Yes, you read that right. People want to work in a place that practices what it preaches.[31]
- A study out of Walden University found that organizations with high levels of integrity experience lower turnover rates and higher levels of employee satisfaction.[32]

It turns out that people like working in a place where honesty is not just a policy but a way of life. Allowing people to bring their real, complete selves to the workplace and giving them the safety to express their ideas, thoughts, and concerns gives rise to greater innovation and a stronger use of creativity.

We need to be seen, heard, and valued to reach our full potential and therefore the potential of our business, our organizations, and our lives. But so many of us are ill-equipped to handle what happens when people show up for work with all their messy lives and selves exposed.

We just don't know how to hold space for being human, until we know.

As you continue on your humanizing way, here are some things to remember, think of, try and explore—rapid fire round style:

Slow down

Slow down,
make room,
generates real connection, and
without it we are always
bouncing off each others'
traumas like bobbleheads wobbling
around all the numbing edges and
we take so damn long to
take a single step or
we rush, all in,
miss the mark,
make partial starts,
release with bugs, and
fix the plane while flying and
instead,
being real, unguarded, and
oh so
human
lets us soften into slowing down
nervous system regulation
coregulate, vagus nerve
grounding, regular beating
hearts bound and
round and round we go,
so to move, with care,
we need to
connect,
slowlysoftly,
in kind.

Cut down your task-based meetings

Ruthlessly cut down on all your project, logistical, and practical meetings. Meetings are only for discussion or decision anyway, and everything else can be done asynchronously. Especially updates. Nobody wants to sit in a meeting and listen to updates. That should've been an e-mail. An hour becomes 45 minutes, 45 minutes becomes 30, and 30 becomes 15.

Expand your emotional meetings

Touchy-feely bits need more space—they're the exact inverse of practical meetings and usually need double the time. An hour needs two, 45 minutes needs an hour and a half, and 30 needs an hour. This will give you the breathing room to sit with the feelings that show up and work through them. And if you finish early, you get a break.

Book your breaks

Put in "no meeting" blocks for lunch, exercise, power naps, and other restorative practices. Humans need to eat and rest. Make time for it.

Ruthlessly limit your work hours

If you're working 60 hours, cut it to 50. Fifty goes to 40. Your 12-hour day goes to 8, 8 goes to 6, and so on. This forces you to focus on what's absolutely necessary and leaves you space for the human things.

A good "no" can be as good as a good "yes."

Get focused

Get focused
on what you will and
will not do
in relationships,
because when
you have looked
yourself straight in
the face and
clearly clarified coordinates on
where your heart and soul meet,
standing strong on the fault lines, loving,
you are much better equipped to
say
no.

As an executive, you can shape the way your business does business—push back on overworking, understaffing, and unreasonable deadlines. Saying no is a skill. It can be very difficult to do it when you are enmeshed with others, people pleasing, flighting, fighting, or fawning your way around your relationships. Good leaders know how to say no to what doesn't work for them, or what they can see isn't going to work for the organization.

Don't just do something, stand there.

Like a good parent, your emotions as a leader will regulate the emotions of others around you. Keep your cool, feel your butt in the chair or your feet on the floor, and take a beat. Breathe first, speak after.

Remember you're all on the same team, trying to do the same things. You can work together.

Wrangling the individuals

Wrangling the individuals
to create the best possible outcomes is
likely the best and hardest part of
humanizing operations but rewarding.
You want to look for those ones with
sparkles, with the momentary leaps of
intuition and a little go with the flow and
less emphasis on short-range thoughts,
profit KPIs, and more on what we're really measuring.
Look for the ways to listen to draw out
all the little personal bits and get to know one another
in dialogue and monologue and talkingthinkingworking and
never never say you want them to
show up and then tell them
"not like that." Either you want it real
and you want all the rewards, or you don't.

Get relational

When someone challenges you or the company, either directly in a con-frontation or indirectly by being themselves, practice Q-Tip first (quit taking it personally) and use that opportunity to listen for the nuggets of change. Remind yourself that your emotions are not their emotions (get some therapy or coaching if this is tough for you). Remember that you don't want them compliant and fitting in—you want them emotionally comfortable and safe enough to share.

Keep learning

Seek out opportunities to hone your relational skills, from your social/emotional intelligence to your collaboration, to systems thinking, commu-nication, and all the other pieces that make your relationships run more smoothly. Get therapy for the things that are sticky and coaching for the things that need gentle holding while you take action to move forward. **If you're not dead, you're not done.**

Keep cleaning it up—your health, your mental game, your bodily main-tenance, your spiritual life, your relationships, and so on. All areas need regular tidying and maintenance and some deep work every once in a while.

Good relationships and

Good relationships and
good relational skills are
the new currency of business
and though they made a bit part
appearance in past series events,
serious, they were never in a
starring role, sidelined.
Now that queries are the furies of the day,
when we know diversity develops
diligent pathways and all
the stats point yes, we need this but,
without those valuable relational skills,
we'll be dead in the water, divided, and so
we'd better learn how to swim.

Extend grace

We make up so many stories when people show up with their whole selves at the table, their emotions on full display and their vulnerability front and center. Instead of judging, get quiet and curious. Ask yourself what the most generous interpretation of their actions and words could be. After all, everyone's doing the best they can with the information they have, and everyone's behavior makes sense to them—at least most of the time! When something looks off on the surface, seek to understand. Instead of dismissing people who don't fit the box, make room for them, and listen, listen, listen.

Disagreement isn't the end

Disagreement isn't the end.
Though the block button looms,
we know that not all fights
are bad
or endless
or reason to leave and
we can disagree on many things,
but work it out,
learn to relate on
a deeper level and
in spite of the fight,
resolve, recover, and
repair
stronger in the cracks, like
kintsuki, golden, and
all the hard conversations lead us
down the road a little further to
understanding one another a
little better and isn't that
isn't that
the way to
a better world?

Whether in the boardroom, the living room, or on the global stage, the ability to navigate disagreements is not just a skill; it is an art.

Getting vulnerable, walking things back, admitting you were wrong, building on the "yes," and saying what you mean, meaning what you say, and opening up to new learning are the paving stones on the path of repair.

Repairing relationships

Repairing relationships
can be quicker than you think,
a simple "I hear you,"
a simple "I'm sorry" and
"what would a good resolution look like?"
goes a long way to mending the rents
that will naturally occur in longtime relations
and more, the stitches of consistent small
good things hold well under strain, and though
trust can be lost, it can be regained.

The true measure of the strength of a relationship lies not in its absence of conflicts but in the ability to navigate and resolve them.

All relationship all the time

All relationship, all the time,
lifemagazine quality, if
you think you aren't
in relationship
you're delusional, illusional!
Even if you're alone romantically,
(why do we think that's the only kind?)
you're not alone,
you're in,
relationship...
with your barista, your
co-workers, your bus riders,
your neighbors, your friends, and
all the people you encounter
in the day, some silent, but
even without eye contact
you're in relationship,
energetic.
If you want to
get anywhere,
do anything,
be anyone,
you must, *must*
learn to relate,
hone your relational skills because
it's not only about technical skill anymore and
you can't hide forever, in fact it's harder to
hide than be seen these days so,
get real about life.
It's all relationship,
all
the
time.

You can only treat people as kindly as you treat yourself.

Once you settle into all your gifts, skills, and talents, you gain more capacity to hold space for and more deeply appreciate others for what they bring to the table and determine how you will relate more carefully to one another moving forward. Gen Z has an advantage on every other generation in this respect, better emotional identification and regulation, better whole picture sense, and they get it, they understand that our world is more than work, and rebel against the idea that 40-hour workweeks in this modern age are necessary for growth and productivity when, naturally, humans are designed to work in short stretches, for enough, not more than we need.

Boomers, Gen X, and Millennials need to catch up.

If you don't have a mentor under 30, you're missing out.

Mentorship is a two-way street now, not just top down and if you're over 40 or 50 or 60, you need the information and coaching that younger people can provide, particularly around emotional intelligence and care. You can help them with their resilience and expertise, but you need them as much as they need you.

Jump the chasm

Jump the chasm,
extend,
yourself outside yourself and
neighboring people, borders broad
influence, persuade, join, and
be
with
is the goal of connection once
you're connected with yourself
plugged in and on, radiating and
like lightning striking two sides of a
canyon bound, energy makes energy,
lit large, immediate circle outside, and
jumping back and forth between
crackling is how
we
connect.

Epilogue

The TikTok phenomenon

The TikTok phenomenon
and going viral
is so much more about
being real and sharing
all the bits and
bobs and nooks and
crannies of yourself
and the things that hit,
hit hard, and
blow up and

(isn't it interesting how all our language is so
violent when it comes to success?)

of all the things we do
that are popular,
lately the most are the
things that are the most
vulnerable,
real,
relatable,
raw,
or just plain funny and
we can be
all of those things,
if we share enough,
nuggets of self, ties
to create a bridge
from my experience
to yours.

Appendixes for My Experienced, Successful Leaders

Hi there. Welcome to your appendixes. I've made them especially for you because I really feel for you. It's not easy to be on top of the world, knowing how everything works and then one day waking up and realizing you're not being listened to like you used to or being challenged on the way business works. You're getting labeled as "dinosaurs" or put in the "old white guys" club or seen as "can-kickers" and it hurts. Nobody likes to be stereotyped or have their ideas dismissed. All my clients who fall into this group of leaders (who I adore) struggle with the changes they're seeing in the corporate world—you're not alone. The good news is that if you're here, you're already on the path—you're willing to read different perspectives and hear other viewpoints. This might feel a bit tough-love, but hopefully this will help. Keep going, we need you!

Appendix 1: Accept That It Might Not Be Your Turn Anymore

No matter how much you might want to help from your place of experience, don't try to do that at first, just wait. Instead, try to see and understand how the paradigm of leadership you've been used to may have caused harm and is shifting. Even if you didn't mean to cause harm, you may have done so (as we all have at different times). You could still be causing it by trying to use past paradigms to solve future issues. Don't worry though, the good news is you're still powerful and so are your peers. You have a role to play in facilitating change, even if it means that you need to move to an advisory seat at the table and out of the lead to let someone else take their turn and try something new.

Appendix 2: Get Used to Being Challenged Differently

Often, my clients have historically leaned on their authority and positional power to shut down challenges (or just didn't have to face them because of their position) but that is becoming increasingly difficult and the challenges are getting stronger. Sometimes, it's hard not to bristle at having your experience, authority, competence, or thinking and behavior challenged, especially if your position has insulated you for a long time. Your first instinct might be to fire back and prove yourself to be right after all, but I encourage you to breathe and try to see the challenge for what it is—a new way of thinking. Be brave, stand there and take the challenge, and be honest about your feelings. It's okay to be challenged, in fact you want people to challenge you and your behavior and thinking. There's no other way to grow.

Appendix 3: Really Listen

When I say listen, I really mean it. Many of my experienced leaders are great problem solvers and doers and sometimes they have to work on simple listening—not listening to jump to solving a problem or to counteract what they're hearing. They sometimes need to listen for context more fully or without ingrained bias. Slow down, try to take in the opinions, perspectives, and emotions you're hearing, and think about how they will apply to your life and your work and the people in your care instead of wanting to sit in the safety of what's always worked for you.

Appendix 4: Swim in a Bigger Pool

How big is your pool? Do you read very different perspectives, or are you only reading your favorite, reliable sources such as the *Wall Street Journal* or *The Harvard Business Review*? Try searching out literature and news from BIPOC creators and from people around the globe. Watch new sources of information like TikTok—the microlearning on that site is incredible and it's accessible to a huge range of creators. You can't expand your pool if you're always taking your comfort zone with you—try to understand different perspectives and ways of being before you dismiss them outright.

Appendix 5: Diversity of Thought Isn't It

This is the first thing I hear people say when they feel uncomfortable with the idea of actual diversity. From my experience, and as you probably know, it can be very tough to engage with people who have a wildly different perspective. The people who push diversity of thought seem very rational—they say that we should be examining problematic behavior and thinking patterns and not worrying so much about actual diversity. I agree in principle that yes, the behaviors and thought patterns need to be addressed, absolutely, but to look only at this misses the larger fact that without diverse people and experiences in a room, you won't get to see truly diverse behavior and thought patterns. You are still selecting behaviors and thoughts from a limited pool.

Appendix 6: Visual Diversity Isn't a Checkbox

I once sat at a table of engineers and executives from a large utility company who were very proud of how well they worked together and they touted their diversity as one of their keys to success. They were visually diverse, with a few women and a couple of people of color on the team. However, on further discussion, it became very apparent that, though they were visually diverse, their life experiences were remarkably similar in terms of schooling, community, career history, religious practice, and other social markers. Simply checking a visual diversity box doesn't mean you'll have real diversity at your table. The table itself needs to adjust to fit new voices.

Appendix 7: Don't Be That Person

The harm comes when you see that there's some old-school thinking and behavior you're engaging in (and perhaps the other experienced leaders around you are engaging in as well) and you don't do anything about it. Don't be that person. Instead, be the person who says, "Why is that funny?" or "Hey, that's offside," or "That doesn't sound right to me," or "Hey, maybe we need to take a different approach here," or "Let's listen here for what we can learn."

Be the change. We need you.

Finally, if you *really* want to extend yourself, make sure your young mentors (more on that in Chapter 9) are very different from you, even the complete opposite; think BIPOC, young, queer, and so on. Go in with a beginner's mind, to every conversation. Let them tell you "how it really is" for them so you can adjust your practices accordingly. Your world isn't the one that's real for them anymore. They face a lot more obstacles than you did, because of the world you helped create. Try to be kind as you listen.

You won't be here forever, and we need you to make room for new voices now while you still have the power.

Thanks for being here.

References

1. Eurich, T. 2018. In *Insight: The Surprising Truth About How Others See us, How We See Ourselves, and Why the Answers Matter More Than We Think*. Crown Currency.
2. Dixon-Fyle, S., K. Dolan, D.V. Hunt, and S. Prince. 2020. In *Diversity Wins: How Inclusion Matters*. McKinsey & Company.
3. Lorenzo, R., N. Voigt, K. Schetelig, A. Zawadzki, I. Welpe, and P. Brosi. 2017. "The Mix That Matters: Innovation Through Diversity." Boston Consulting Group.
4. Volini, E., J. Schwartz, B. Denny, D. Mallon, Y. Van Durme, M. Hauptmann, R. Yan, and S. Poynton. 2020. "The Social Enterprise at Work: Paradox as a Path Forward." Deloitte.
5. Klofstad, C.A., R.C. Anderson, and S. Peters. July 7, 2012. "Sounds Like a Winner: Voice Pitch Influences Perception of Leadership Capacity in Both Men and Women." In *Proceedings of the Royal Society B: Biological Sciences*, p. 279.
6. Tsantani, M.S., P. Belin, H.M. Paterson, and P. McAleer. 2016. "Low Vocal Pitch Preference Drives First Impressions Irrespective of Context in Male Voices but not in Female Voices." *Perception* 45, no. 8, pp. 946–963.
7. Boyle, M. and J. Green. 2023. "Work Shift: Women CEOs (Finally) Outnumber Those Named John." Bloomberg.
8. Roberts-Gibson, K., D. Harari, and J. Carson-Marr. 2018. "When Sharing Hurts: How and Why Self-Disclosing Weakness Undermines the Task-Oriented Relationships of Higher Status Disclosers." *Organizational Behavior and Human Decision Processes 144,* no. 1, pp. 25–43.
9. Anonymous. 2017. "What I Wish I Could Tell My Boss: 'Telling You About My Mental Health Was a Big Mistake'." The Guardian.
10. Marshburn, C.K., K.J. Cochran, E. Flynn, L.J. Levine. 2020. "Workplace Anger Costs Women Irrespective of Race." *Frontiers in Psychology Personality and Social Psychology* 11.

11. Chen, L., and V. Menon. 2018. "Positive Attitude Toward Math Predicts Math Achievement in Kids." *Psychological Science.*

12. Pew Research Center. 2023. In *Diversity, Equity and Inclusion in the Workplace.*

13. Piff, P., D. Keltner, D. Stancato, and S. Cote. 2012. "Higher Social Class Predicts Increased Unethical Behavior." *PNAS* 109, no. 11.

14. Northrup, K. 2019. In *Do Less.* Hay House Inc.

15. Kantor, J., K. Weise, and G. Ashford. 2021. "Inside Amazon's Worst Human Resources Problem." *New York Times.*

16. Kantor, J., K. Weise, and G. Ashford. 2021. "What We Learned About Amazon's Warehouse Workers." *New York Times.*

17. "Federal Social Safety Net Programs: Millions of Full-Time Workers Rely on Federal Health Care and Food Assistance Programs." 2020. US Government Accountability Office. www.gao.gov/products/gao-21-45.

18. Mitchell, J. and K. Dill. 2021. "Workers Quit Jobs in Droves to Become Their Own Bosses." *Wall Street Journal.*

19. Raworth, K. 2017. "A Doughnut for the Anthropocene: Humanity's Compass in the 21st century." *The Lancet* 1, no. 2.

20. Centers for Disease Control and Prevention. 2021. "Making the Business Case for Total Worker Health." National Institute for Occupational Safety and Health, Total Worker Health.

21. Ellingrud, K., S. Sanghvi, G.S. Dandona, A. Madgavkar, M. Chui, O. White, and P. Hasebe. 2023. In *Generative AI and the Future of Work in America.* McKinsey Global Institute.

22. Gallup Research. 2013. *The Benefits of Employee Engagement.*

23. Boushey, H. and S.J. Glynn. 2012. "There Are Significant Costs to Replacing Employees." American Progress.

24. Baldoni, J. 2013, "Employee Engagement Does More Than Boost Productivity." *Harvard Business Review.*

25. Oswald, A.J., E. Proto, and D. Sgroi. 2009. "Happiness and Productivity." *Journal of Labor Economics.*

26. Jelinek, C. and R. Vachris. 2022. "Costco Wholesale 2022 Annual Report."

27. Mobius, M. and T. Rosenblat. 2006. "Why Beauty Matters." *American Economic Review* p. 96.

28. Hamermesh, D.S., J.E. Biddle. 1994. "Beauty and the Labour Market." *American Economic Review* p. 84.

29. Riborg-Mann, C. 1918. In *A Study of Engineering Education*. Carnegie Foundation.

30. Kaliski, J., T. Bernhardt-Lanier, M. Ferrari, and M.L. Chen. "The Purpose Premium: Why a Purpose-Driven Strategy Is Good for Business." Deloitte Monitor.

31. Glassdoor Consulting. 2019. *Mission and Culture Survey 2019*. www.glassdoor.com/blog/mission-culture-survey/.

32. Osborne, S. and M.S. Hammoud. 2017. "Effective Employee Engagement in the Workplace." *International Journal of Applied Management and Technology* p. 16.

About the Author

Katherine Lazaruk is a professional presence expert who helps leaders and their teams walk the walk, talk the talk, and look the part. She is passionate about achieving gender parity in her lifetime and through her coaching, consulting, and speaking, and she works with women and champions of women to get more women into senior leadership faster. Recognizing that we are currently in a shifting paradigm, she works within the system to change the system for teams and individuals alike to create a kinder, gentler, and more effective world.

Katherine holds degrees in Voice Performance and Education and holds her second-level international designation of Certified Image Professional (CIP) with the Association of Image Consultants International (AICI) and her Professional Certified Coach (PCC) designation with the International Coach Federation (ICF). She has also been Vice Chair of the Women's Leadership Council Advisory Committee with the Greater Vancouver Board of Trade and served for six years as the Secretary of the AICI Canada Chapter Board. She has been a member of the nominations committee for the YWCA Vancouver Women of Distinction Awards and volunteered with two of their programs for women, sharing her expertise on professional presence, and currently, she serves on the Global Diversity, Equity, and Inclusion Committee for AICI.

Katherine lives in Vancouver and spends her spare time singing jazz, opera, and vintage big band music, songwriting, and publishing books of "long stories in short poems" (katherinelazaruk.com). She can be found hanging out at concerts and movies with her husband and her wide circle of friends or playing a board game or two at home, sipping a craft cocktail. She enjoys challenging conversations, is relentlessly curious, and can be slightly irreverent from time to time.

Index

OTHER TITLES IN THE CORPORATE COMMUNICATION COLLECTION

Debbie Dufrene, Stephen F. Austin State University, Editor

- *Internal Communication in the Age of Artificial Intelligence* by Monique Zytnik
- *Ensuring Civility Online* by Virginia Hemby
- *Win Business with Relationships* by May Hongmei Gao
- *101 Tips for Improving Your Business Communication* by Edward Barr
- *How to Become a Master of Persuasion* by Tony Treacy
- *The Thong Principle* by donalee Moulton
- *Business Writing For Innovators and Change-Makers* by Dawn Henwood
- *New Insights into Prognostic Data Analytics in Corporate Communication* by Pragyan Rath and Kumari Shalini
- *Delivering Effective Virtual Presentations* by K. Virginia Hemby
- *Technical Marketing Communication, Second Edition* by Emil B. Towner and Heidi L. Everett
- *Zen and the Art of Business Communication* by Susan L. Luck
- *Fundamentals of Writing for Marketing and Public Relations* by Janet Mizrahi
- *Managing Investor Relations* by Alexander Laskin
- *Managerial Communication* by J. David Johnson
- *Communication in Responsible Business* by Roger N. Conaway and Oliver Laasch

Concise and Applied Business Books

The Collection listed above is one of 30 business subject collections that Business Expert Press has grown to make BEP a premiere publisher of print and digital books. Our concise and applied books are for...

- Professionals and Practitioners
- Faculty who adopt our books for courses
- Librarians who know that BEP's Digital Libraries are a unique way to offer students ebooks to download, not restricted with any digital rights management
- Executive Training Course Leaders
- Business Seminar Organizers

Business Expert Press books are for anyone who needs to dig deeper on business ideas, goals, and solutions to everyday problems. Whether one print book, one ebook, or buying a digital library of 110 ebooks, we remain the affordable and smart way to be business smart. For more information, please visit www.businessexpertpress.com, or contact sales@businessexpertpress.com.